BACKPACKERS & FLASHPACKERS IN EASTERN EUROPE:

500 Hostels In 100 Cities In 25 Countries

HARDIE KARGES

ISBN: 0988490528

ISBN 13: 9780988490529

Library of Congress Control Number: 2012919937
Hypertravel Books, Los Angeles, California

Table of Contents

Table of Contents

Preface: Confessions Of An Aging Backpacker

Okay, okay, I admit it. I like to travel; no more long-winded explanations about business, "raw material," or "I like interesting places, but not the actual traveling to get there." I like it all, okay? It's a way of life—the spontaneity, the breeze in your hair, the new experience just around the next bend, the friend-for-life that you just might meet tomorrow. Who says you have to sit in a little house on a little street in a little town in a little country every day for the rest of your life anyway? My Indo-European-speaking ancestors certainly didn't. They spread far and wide with nothing much more than a herd of cattle for inspiration. Those humble herders went on to become Greeks, Romans, Persians, Russians, Germans, French, British, and Americans. And what's the first thing those modern men and women want to do when they're old enough to leave home and have enough money to consider their options? For many, the answer is obvious: travel. Like salmon swimming upriver, maybe it's there in the genes somewhere.

For a backpacker luxury is not the goal. Adventure is; or if not true adventure, then at least novelty. A true backpacker will go hundreds of miles out of his way to cross a border that's only recently opened and the people are not yet jaded. That's virgin territory; but we can change all that. This is what I call the Backpacker Uncertainty Principle: that undiscovered paradise at the end of that new road will be altered by our very presence; and our own perceptions are only that, not reality itself. Still we persist in our search for novelty. This is, after all, the greatest show on earth, in full Technicolor, Sensurround, and Odorama. You're only limited by your imagination and your pocketbook. Of course if you're a true backpacker, it doesn't take much money. It takes smarts, and a modicum of daring. There's only one guiding Backpacker Rule and it's simple: *Travel light.* Okay, you don't have to drill holes in your toothbrush as one early travel guide jokingly suggested, but you get the idea.

For better or worse, back when I first started, there was no Lonely Planet travel guide, much less hundreds, much less Rough Guide, Moon Publications, or any of the others. Standards were the Frommer books and the series based on "Europe on $10 a Day." South American Handbook was the Bible for Latin America and there were just starting to be some "cool" travel books coming out like "Southeast Asia on a Shoestring," "Indonesia Handbook," "Along the Gringo Trail," and "People's Guide to Mexico." The last of these was probably my all-time favorite, simply because it told you nothing about where to stay or what to pay, but it told you what it's like to be part of the landscape. For me, ultimately, that's what it's all about. I know what it's like being a tourist, backpacker or otherwise. That's nearly the same everywhere. Guesthouses, restaurants, and travel agencies, even mountains, rivers, and deserts are very similar all over the world.

Cultures are what distinguish a place. I want to know what it's like to live there. That's what we backpackers do. We live in a series of situations linked like a chain, neither constant travelling nor constant residence. Sure, I want to know where the temples, museums, and waterfalls are, but I also want to know what's in the nightclubs, movie theatres and markets, also. A book doesn't help much with that, and I used to eschew them religiously. Now I eschew them because I hardly know where I'll end up when I start out, and extra paper violates Backpacker Rule #1.

I like to think of myself as one of the "originals," but actually I'm not. I started in the mid-70's, what I would call the "belated Hippie" era. That was probably the Golden Age, when many places in the world were still inexpensive, still culturally distinguishable, but developed enough, and globally aware enough, that accommodations catering to this youthful group had already sprung up, almost overnight in some cases. A Westerner could simply hop on the bus and cross on over to the other side. For an American, that meant Mexico and South America. For a European, that meant Turkey and Africa. For an Australian or Japanese, Indonesia and Southeast Asia were obvious choices. For all, India was like the jewel in the crown, prized equally for its guru-laden culture and long-time facility with the English language. India, indeed, was the favorite of the previous generation that started out as beatniks in Goa, Tangier, and Ajijic and ended up as hippies smelling the roses in Kathmandu, Marrakesh, and Panajachel. The scene changed from the beatnik characters portrayed in *On the Road* and progressed to the hippies of *Great Railway Bazaar* to the post-hippies of *Video Night in Kathmandu* to the slackers of *The Beach* to the modern-day flashpackers of *Hypertravel.*

Of course the backpacker scene changes all the time, by definition. Old places lose their charm and new places open for business, many times due to political considerations. Laos was in, out, now back in, ditto for Siem Reap, but give Kabul a little more time. Vietnam still lures, Yangshuo and Dali in China still maintain their charm even after the novelty's gone, and Tallinn is the rockingest spot in Europe, long after Western Europe almost priced itself out of the backpacker market. Sometimes an area or city remains popular, but the center for backpackers drifts to new neighborhoods. Kathmandu's Freak Street has moved across town to Thamel, as has Bangkok's Soi Ngam Duphli to Khaosan Road, while Bali's Kuta Beach merely extends itself endlessly down the same street, first to Legian, then to Seminyak, like growth rings on a tree. Rising prices, along with increased crime, have decreased the attraction of Latin America, but there are still adventures to be had, especially in the South American Andes.

The threat of violence also affects perceptions of Africa and Muslim countries, but persevere. If you don't mind being the only backpacker around, then every place is a potential trip. You don't really require banana pancakes, do you? Asia is clearly "Easy Street" for today's backpackers, what with former Communist countries not only cheap, not only time capsules, but now allowing multiple entry and exit points so that one can loop back to a starting point without re-tracing one's steps. This is Backpacker Rule #2 (Okay, I lied earlier): *Backpack, don't backtrack.* Novelty is worth the long hard bumpy ride through uncertainty and digestive distress, but reruns only excite when they're nostalgia runs, like time travel, same space but different times. But that takes a few years to be effective.

Yes, things have certainly changed since that day almost forty years ago when I first put thumb to the air and the rest was history. Gone is the Culture Shock. Gone is the thumb, as a rule of thumb. Gone are the days of "going native," when you'd trade your jeans, Vibram-soled boots and down-filled jacket for the local handspun and go live in a hovel with the Indians. I suppose that is a testament to the increasing globalization of world culture, but probably also to the increasing luxury of the backpacker scene. Backpackers now have got it easy, what with all the centers of cheap accommodation competing for your dollar, all the cafes, all the guidebooks, all the Modern Standard Pidgin English gone worldwide. But I'm not complaining. I got a glimpse of a past they'll never get. I became a self-taught linguist out of the necessities of world travel. I became a self-taught anthropologist to try to make sense of everything I saw. I even made a career out of travel, dealing in handicrafts when they, too, had a novelty value and a Golden Age which is now in decline. I've even had the opportunity to live in several foreign countries (and still be my own boss).

Internet makes travel much easier and knowledgeable nowadays. E-tickets mean you don't have to worry about losing that handful of tickets that link you back to the "real world." Improved transportation means that formerly inaccessible areas are now open for business, notwithstanding the fact that what attracted you in the first place may change in the process. Life is good. I've visited one hundred forty-five countries (and counting), worked in ten or twelve of them, and lived in two or three of them. AND THEY'RE CREATING NEW ONES ALL THE TIME. I figure if I visit five or six new countries a year, then I'll see them all before, well, you know. I still barely know Africa, and soon Central Asia will be my main game to play. Forget those obscure land borders, though.

At fifty-eight years old (and counting), I start looking for airlines from exotic countries that allow free stopovers at no extra cost. I start looking to see which airlines make fuel stops in Cape Verde. I start weighing the options of flying from Bangkok to New York via the Pacific or Atlantic. I start seeing the world not as a random collection of countries, but as Hispanic, Germanic, Francophone, Lusophone, Slavic, Semitic, Uralic, Altaic, Bantu, Manchu, Sino-Tibetan, or Uto-Aztecan, etc. according to the historical ebb and flow of peoples, religions, languages, and power. I stop counting the years and start counting my blessings. Unfortunately, I still need to count my money.

What we didn't have back then—except for some places in Europe—were hostels. But those weren't necessarily geared towards backpackers. Those were usually geared towards students. Still the many inexpensive lodgings on newly-opened trails were very similar to what hostels represent today—places to trade info, stories, knowledge, and if the mood is right, maybe even body fluids. Travel is supposed to be fun, after all, and if the typical backpacker is more interested in remoteness and authenticity than whining and dining, still that ultimate objective of communion with *the other* is common to all travel experiences. Unfortunately it can all be a bit chaotic and confusing, so I'm trying to make some sense of it all here. See you in Sarajevo. See you in a hostel.

Introduction

What is a hostel? Originally they were places, mostly in Europe, where students could sleep for cheap on extended country outings, frequently established at appropriate intervals over and about the landscape and which corresponded more or less to the amount of distance a student might hike or bike in the course of a day. Since those outings usually occurred in the summer when schools were otherwise uncommitted, the schools themselves became the logical place for seasonal conversion. That still happens sometimes, but not much. The concept has expanded dramatically over the last decade, for a variety of reasons, no doubt; among them: rising hotel prices, rising restaurant prices, and—drum roll here, please—Internet. For the rise of Internet has not only made advance booking widely accessible for both hostel and traveler, but it also became a reasonably-priced accommodation where a traveler would almost certainly have access to that same Internet. This fueled an explosion which is still happening to this day, and has barely scratched the surface yet in many places.

In the introduction to my book "Hypertravel: 100 Countries in 2 Years," I wrote, "Not surprisingly, hostels are least prevalent in places where cheap hotels and guest houses are most available, such as Southeast Asia." I just might have to return the Cuban cigar I received for that brilliant observation. At last count Singapore had over forty hostels, and even very-reasonably-priced Bangkok almost as many. In contrast Boston, in the good ol' US of A, has… what, two or three? I guess hostels, with their shared rooms, just aren't American. But all that's changing, especially in New York, with some of the highest hotel rates in the world. Even in Africa, especially southern Africa, the concept is huge and growing, and in Latin America, they're fairly abundant. The only problem is that there exists something of a flexible and locally-influenced definition of what really makes a good hostel, so that this guide to East European hostels will reflect those considerations.

What any good hostel should have, by my own current standards, are: 1) cheap dorm beds, 2) English language, 3) a kitchen, 4) storage lockers, and

5) easy access to Internet. Of course within each of those categories there exists significant margin for deviation, but a place of lodging should make the effort to at least offer something in each of these five basic requirements in my humble opinion. Other things you can expect that probably wouldn't be considered "amenities" include DIY bedding (you know how to make a bed, right?) and the likely absence of a towel (though many have it, but charge). For purposes of this guide I had to decide what ultimately defines a hostel, and for me that's the shared rooms. It's nice, for me at least, if they have private rooms also, but if they don't have dorms, then they won't be in this book. This book is not intended to be comprehensive, so don't be surprised if you don't see your favorite party hostel in Belgrade. This book tries to be selective. There's a reason for that, several of them, in fact.

There are some downsides with hostels in general, though usually no more than the sometimes institutional nature of them. A bigger problem can be location, especially where they're rare. That hostel may be located far from the center and not obvious even when standing right in front of it, no sign of the business conducted within, many of them no doubt informal in their business approach. There are other issues, also, such as the once-standard curfews which are rapidly disappearing. Then there are the also-once-standard age limits, also in decline, though still there, the main problem being one of where to draw the line. I've seen upper limits anywhere between thirty-five and fifty-five. That's problematic for those of us who hold non-discrimination dearly *and who are already over fifty-five.*

Other hostels are more creative and limit ages only within dorm rooms. That sounds reasonable, especially given the other discrimination issue: most dorms are of mixed sexes, though female-only dorms are not uncommon. It's mostly cool and without problems, but still these are valid issues to consider. Most backpackers' hostels simply have no age limit, and that's the way it should be, I feel. Any problems can be dealt with on an individual basis. Another related problem is that in some cities of Europe hostel beds rank as decent long-term accommodations for some individuals and even families, who attempt to live there. Most hostels rightfully attempt to discourage this, as they should. Hostels are not transient hotels, after all. I try to weed those places out.

It gets worse. Some small hostels are barely staffed, if at all, absentee landlords showing up to let you in and set you up, then disappearing until the next guest shows up. Many legitimate "boutique" hotels do that, too, especially in northern Europe, where they rightfully value their own private lives, but others are merely renting a flat and calling it a hostel, with little regard to your needs or that of their neighbors. If you book in advance, and they demand to know your arrival time, then that's a good clue. If they call you in advance, that's another. If they have no website and the hostel-booking site has few pictures, then that's another. Unfortunately a place with a bad rep can simply change its name and start all over as if nothing ever happened. I try to weed those places out of this guide and include only "real" hostels. With this guide you can contact hostels directly before committing any money, which is good. That way you can do some weeding, too, even at the last minute. You can't do that with most hostel-booking sites, which for many hostels is their only connection to potential customers.

For better or worse, consolidation is setting in to the hostel scene rapidly, and the days of the "hippie hostel" may be numbered. The most obvious manifestation of this trend is the appearance of hostel chains, not only within a city or country, but in multiple cities across a region, especially Western Europe. I think that this in general is good, as it establishes standards of services and expectations. The downside, that quirky little mom-and-pop operations may get squeezed out, is probably misplaced, since many of those places wouldn't rate very highly on my hostel-meter anyway, and the current "Air BnB" trend is probably more suitable to their offerings. Many of those would not even be found in this book, since they don't have websites. Conversely, many of the biggest chains will not be represented for every one of their branches here. I try to strike a balance between standards and individuality. Just because a place calls itself a hostel is not enough for me.

A word should be mentioned about HI, Hostelling International, which is often affiliated with YHA and such. This is the original hostel chain, and largely responsible for the existence of hostels, or at least their smooth transition from those early schoolboy barracks into modern backpackers' party hostels. They are a membership organization and you will need to pay an extra charge to stay there if you're not a member. When you've done this a half-dozen times or so, you'll be a member. But this guide is not about HI, though some are listed, particularly the ones that offer beds on the major hostel-booking sites. In fact they could probably fill a book larger than this of only their member hostels worldwide, though many of their branches are open only seasonally, so I won't concentrate much on them. For better or worse, they tend to represent the old school of "youth hostels" more than the modern era of backpackers and flashpackers.By the way in some quarters a hostel itself is known as a "backpackers," short for "backpackers' hostel," I assume. Make a note. Also, pricing gets elaborate and confusing, and frequently changing, so are included here for comparison purposes only. Just know that in Western Europe a dorm bed will likely run $20-50 and in Eastern Europe somewhat less, maybe as little as half that. And for a private room, you'll have to pay that same price for two to three people, regardless of how many actually occupy the room. You should be aware that in some places—London comes to mind—you might do better price-wise for a small cramped private room in one of the chock-a-block centers of budget accommodation around Earl's Court, Victoria Coach Station, or Shepherd's Bush. That's when some of the other considerations come in, like Wi-Fi or a kitchen or…

The best thing about a hostel I've hardly even mentioned yet, because it's a hard thing to quantify, and that's the people you'll meet. Even an old geezer like me needs some social intercourse (yep) from time to time, and given our frequent differences from the locals, travelers are the next best thing. In out-of-the-way places like Armenia or Namibia, that's priceless. In places like London, that's "Party Time!" Don't forget to wear protection (for your ears, that is). So that's pretty much what hostels aka "backpackers" are all about. But what's a "flashpacker," you ask? I think that's what you become when you've been a backpacker too long and can't stop, maybe a little older, hopefully a little wiser, more up-scale and maybe less group-oriented, i.e. hard-core, or maybe 'die-hard.' I guess that's me. Some flashpackers may also be more urban and less interested in remote locations than in partying in the pubs. That's not me.

If you're American, then you're probably wondering why this historic trend seems to have skipped over the good ol' USA. Actually it didn't, really. Ever heard of the YMCA? They're always booked up in New York. This book's for you. America's indeed the last to get in on the modern trend, but I expect that to change very soon. I think many Americans just can't see themselves staying in dorms, but that's half the fun if you're young, and a surefire way to meet people. So what makes this book better than a website for booking hostels? That's like comparing apples and oranges. For one thing, we give you the hostel's own website and/or e-mail address and phone number for direct communication. So, not only can we be more objective than a booking site that receives a commission, but a booking site may show a hostel to be full when a call or e-mail to the hostel itself will get you a bed immediately. For another, we try to include only the "real" hostels, hopefully without bad reviews. But if they don't have dorms, then they won't be here, and likely the same result if they have no website.

This is intended as an introduction and complement to the vast online resources and hopefully a broader view. Still, hostel-booking sites are invaluable for feedback, specific information and special promotions, and I urge everyone to consult them. Two of the bigger ones that I know best are *www.hostelbookers.com* and *www.hostelworld.com*, though there are many others, and *www.hostelz.com* acts as something of a "kayak" for them all, so that's good. Then there's the membership-only *www.hihostels.com*, but as mentioned before, that's more likely an old-school "youth hostel," so not really the focus here, though some are included. If you're looking for something out in the countryside, they may even be best. But we're getting ahead of ourselves. This is a travel guide (both time and space), as well as a hostel guide. If you're a novice traveler, then you need to know some basics first.

Travel Basics & Traveling Around Eastern Europe

Transportation: Buses, Trains, & Planes

There's nothing more basic to travel than the actual transportation. In general that means buses, trains, and planes, right? Well, for international travel, especially inter-continental travel, that mostly means planes. But which planes? Well, you can just go to a travel agent and they'll be happy to do everything for you, but if you're a do-it-yourselfer like me, then you probably want a little bit more control over the process than that, and you probably wouldn't mind knowing how it works, so that you can tweak it to your own tastes and proclivities. The good news is that with online booking you can do that. I do things in the booking process I wouldn't dare ask an agent to do. The first thing to decide is where and when you want to go, and then start pricing.

First determine what's the nearest major hub city (usually the largest and the lowest price) in the region you're going to, or coming from, and then compare to that. Major hubs around the world include London, Paris, Cairo, Istanbul, Dubai, Johannesburg, Delhi, Bangkok, Singapore, Lima, and others. In the US: New York, LA, San Francisco, Chicago, Miami, Houston, Dallas and Atlanta are the biggies, in no certain order. If you're traveling abroad and want a multi-city route, then carefully check for airlines that hub in one of the cities on your route, for instance for LA-Paris-Cairo-LA, you'll definitely want to check Egyptair and Air France, in addition to a multi-line site or two. Expedia and the like can and will book any multi-segment flight on multiple airlines, very convenient!

Are you still with me? So what's next? In the old days I'd check the Sunday travel section in LA, New York, or San Fran papers—the library'd have them if the newsstands didn't—and start looking for deals from "bucket shops," i.e. consolidators. They'd buy large blocks of seats to re-sell and always undercut the airlines themselves, who were limited by IATA rules and regs in what they could do. Then I'd get on the 800# line and start chatting with someone with a thick accent in Times Square or Union Square or Chinatown or on Broadway downtown somewhere, trying to get the right price. It'd never be the price in the ad, of course, but I'd try to get close. Then I'd make payment and ticketing arrangements to be mailed back and forth, money order for them, paper ticket usually Fedexed to me, very "old school." Or if I were stopping in that same city on my way out of the country, then I might even stop in their office, if I could squeeze into the cramped spaces they typically occupied. Those ads have mostly disappeared.

It's easier than that now. Some of those places still exist—Flight Center and STA Travel come to mind as multi-city biggies—but rarely will they have better deals now than what you could find for yourself on the Net. I usually go to one of the major multi-airline travel sites like Expedia, Travelocity, etc. (or Kayak will pull them all up for you to compare) and see who flies where and when for how much. Then I'll go to the website of one or more of those airlines and compare prices. They're not always the same, and as often as not the multi-airline site will be cheaper, BUT… that might change tomorrow. The airline's own site will change less, but the multi-line sites can somehow magically splice together several airlines for multi-city itineraries, all at very reasonable prices. They also have hotels, too, but if you're reading this book, then that's probably not your thing. One advantage to Expedia, etc. is that prices include tax; with airlines' own sites, you'll probably have to continue to checkout. Don't be fooled by false low numbers.

When to buy? You know that already, don't you? The sooner you buy, the better the price, right? Not necessarily. Of course you need to check as far in advance as possible just to budget yourself, but I'd say start checking prices seriously no later than three months before your anticipated travel date. But don't buy yet. Online sales are usually immediate, so you probably want to keep options open as long as you can. A travel agent might make a reservation for you and let you pay later, so that's one advantage to working with them. Then if you find it cheaper yourself, you can cancel with the agent or simply let it expire. Don't book the same flight as the one your agent's already booked, though. That gets messy.

I'd still advise you to do some legwork, regardless. If your dates are flexible, then check prices for each day a week before and after your preferred date; they'll probably vary, but Tuesday and Wednesday will usually be cheapest. Check again a week later; it goes fast when you get the hang of it. If prices start going up for Fridays then you might want to go ahead and purchase that Wednesday flight. If not, then wait. I've seen some major discounts right at two months out, if the seats aren't selling quickly enough, so wait until then if you can, fifty-nine days out if your plans are firm enough. If not then start monitoring every day or two. A large group can sell a flight out quickly. Once a seat is gone, they rarely come back. It's not like the old days when reservations were made, then frequently cancelled.

If you're trying to book a frequent-flyer flight from an airline, generally a tiered system will charge you a certain amount of miles for Europe (50K+/-), Asia (75K+/-), Africa (100K+/-), etc. without any advantage necessarily to the major hubs. Those hubs may have stiffer fees and taxes, too, and the award usually doesn't cover that. I'm searching flights to Africa from the US right now, hubbing out of Europe. It costs 40,000 frequent-flyer miles to fly to either London or Lisbon. London's fees are $600; Lisbon's are $200. Go figure. If you're using frequent-flyer miles attached to a major non-airline bank card, then usually now those convert to 1% of the cost of the flight, i.e. 50,000 miles = $500 flight, booking through their agent. Poke around the site first, though, and you might find a minor partner that still uses the old tier system (like Bank of America's Canadian partner). You'll likely get more that way if you're flexible with dates. Whew!

To fly to East Europe it might be cheaper to fly in to West Europe first, and then catch a cheap flight or Eurolines bus to East Europe. Wizz Air in Poland is good, and Poland is not a bad place to hub out of, with easy connections all around. Flights to Moscow are among the cheapest to Europe, somewhat mitigating the visa hassles, but Moscow is only good as a hub to the rest of Russia, not other countries, since you'd need a double-entry visa then to fly back out. Trains are well-established there, though, so something of a throwback to West Europe, or a bygone age. Except for Russia, or unless you are traveling to or from West Europe also, then buses will probably be easier to find than trains. Most countries have budget airlines also, though, so it's worth a check. They can often be ridiculously cheap.

Visas: Consulates, Passports, & Letters of Introduction

Depending on your nationality and where you're going, you might need a visa, which is a stamp in your passport that is your permit to enter a specific country. They have to be applied for at an embassy or a consulate. Do that two to three months before travel, also, if possible. You already knew you needed a passport, right? Don't worry; it can usually all be done by mail, but allow plenty of time, and make sure your passport has at least six months of validity from the date you plan to enter the last country on your itinerary or they might not let you in. Visas can sometimes be picked up on the road, but get as many as you can in advance from your home, especially if you live in a major city that has embassies and consulates. Nothing is certain out there. There are companies that will do it for you, but it can get quite expensive. Google hard, but the best source for knowing what visas you'll need (if you're American) is probably *http://travel.state.gov*. Other countries have their own. If you're doing the work yourself, then check the websites of the countries whose visa you need to get instructions.

For Eastern Europe, you'll need visas for Russia and Belarus, and they're a real pain-in-the-ass, too, expensive and confusing and requiring "letters of invitation." Specialized travel agents can do that for you, so you might as well get them to do your visa, also. Once you get there, there are hotel registrations, too. Unless you just gotta' see Moscow or St. Pete or have a ticket for the Siberian train, or are going to every country like me, then I can hardly recommend it, frankly. The Ukraine is a big beautiful friendly cheap substitute in my humble opinion, no visa required. Oh yeah, Turkey and the Caucasus countries—Armenia, Georgia, and Azerbaijan—require visas also, but they are available at the border, so no big deal. As of this date, that means only at the airport for Azerbaijan, land borders also okay for the other countries. If you're coming back through, ask about "multiple-entry." If you're buzzing right through (three days or less), ask about "transit visas." And read the actual visa. It might be good for multiple entries, even though you didn't know it (Turkey).

Money: Currencies, Exchange Rates, and ATM's

Money is important when traveling, of course, the more the better, but you don't have to actually carry it all with you. In general I recommend ATM's, since traveler's checks are almost extinct, and you usually have to go into a bank to cash them, as opposed to the generally more available exchange booths. The problem with ATM's is that they aren't everywhere in the world, believe it or not, and service charges can be high. If you plan to travel a lot, it's worth getting a bank account that doesn't charge much for foreign transactions. You need cash, too, of course, and a credit card for emergencies, so I recommend a mix of them all, a few traveler's checks, too, if you've got them. You don't want to get stuck with extra foreign currency, though Euros or Pounds are not so bad since easily changeable almost everywhere. There's an art to using up your worthless currency. Buy gifts at the end of a trip to use up extra currency. The last few days change just what you need until you cross the next border. Small denomination dollars (or whatever your currency) are good for those border areas.

Change money at established locations unless you're desperate, and count your money carefully whether at an exchange house, at a bank, or on the street. But first look at the posted rates, both of them. There's a "buying" rate and a "selling" rate. Unless you're leaving the country and want dollars or Euros or whatever back, then the buying rate is the one you're getting, the lower of the two. If it's a good rate, then there should be no more than 2-3% difference between the two. If it's more than five I'd probably pass, unless I'm desperate. Also check to see if there are commissions or extra charges. In Western Europe there usually are. Use ATM's. Use any leftover currency immediately at the border or first stop of the new country you're entering, or you might be stuck with it. Some currencies are non-convertible, e.g. Belarusian rubles. Use 'em up. Never exchange money at a US airport on the way out. It's a rip-off, same in West Europe. If I need to carry cash in US Dollars, then I usually prefer fifty-dollar-bills, since they'll get as good of a rate as hundreds, are usually prettier, and are easier to cash in a pinch. Old worn bills won't pass.

Most East European countries still have their own currency, though a few use the Euro, so change small amounts. Euro is the best currency to hold in quantity, followed by dollars and pounds sterling. Small-denomination US bills can sometimes be used at borders and with taxis for those last-minute unexpected charges. There are no small denomination Euro or pound sterling bills. Coins are useless outside their own countries. Use 'em up. Most East European countries' own paper notes are not much better, changeable only at poor rates, if at all, beyond the immediate border. Use 'em or lose 'em.

Communications: Cell-phones, Cards & Computers

I think this is where the phrase, "it's complicated," originates. If you're European or from most anywhere else in the world besides the US, then it's easier. But America is slow to get on the worldwide GSM digital network standard for cell phones, and that's what you need, that and a multi-band phone, one that can handle both 1900 (Am) and 1800 (rest of world) band frequencies. Most new phones will make the switch automatically; if not, then look in the menu for something like settings>network>band, and then choose the one you need. If you're already with AT&T, T-Mobile or another GSM network in the US, then your phone should work all around the world, albeit with high international roaming charges. You may need to activate world service first. Poke around the website, though, and you might find some special arrangements for particular countries. Barring that, if you're going to be in any one country for very long, then it's worth buying a local SIM card and putting it in your phone.

What's a SIM card? Simply put: that little thumbnail-size circuit-board accessible through the back of the phone is your number and all the information that goes with it, including your calling history. It's easy to switch, but you'll probably have to "unlock" your phone first if it's American. American cell-phone services are traditionally monopolized, with prices to match. If that's what it takes to produce iPhones, then so be it. If you're switching services in the US, then request the company to unlock it. If you're tech-savvy, you might even find tools online to unlock it yourself. Otherwise, go to the sleazy part of town in some sleazy city (say, London) where people do things they're not supposed to do and look for signs around cell-phone shops that say "phones unlocked," or something like that. Buy a local SIM card for ten or fifteen bucks, stick it in, and then start blabbing. Some might even be worth keeping, if they give you a better international rate than your US phone would.

Smart phones are too new for me to have the skinny worldwide. Buy the next edition, and I'll promise to be up-to-date by then. This is a real breakthrough, obviously, to have a local map in your hands constantly and ready to use. It's not that easy, though, not yet anyway. For one thing, there are the high roaming fees mentioned earlier. For another, the G3 system doesn't exist everywhere in the world yet, much less G4, so simply buying a new SIM card and sticking it in is not necessarily a quick easy solution. Stay tuned. As a lover of maps, I find this development exciting if only for that reason. After all, who do I want to call in most countries that I travel in? But maps are something else entirely.

Actually phone-cards are still popular and useful, but you don't always need actual cards. Sometimes all you need are the PIN number and the access numbers, so you can do that online with much greater choice than in Chinatown. Ones that allow you to call all over the world from the US are dirt cheap. Cards that allow calling from anywhere to everywhere might be harder to find and more expensive. Read the fine print carefully. Of course even then you'll need a local phone to call the access number, so maybe not worth the hassle for a traveler.

The more modern alternative is to use Skype on your Internet device: anywhere everywhere cheap no hassle, all you need is WiFi for calling out or even receiving calls whenever you happen to be online. For someone to call you anywhere any time, though, you still need your own number. Skype rates may finally be climbing now, but there are copycats with similar services to compare to. As for Internet in general, Wi-Fi is an international standard, so available everywhere, of course, but don't expect them to be everywhere for free. Since you're reading this book, though, your odds are very good with the places listed here. One nice thing about G-4 cell-phone-style Internet is that it'll be everywhere there's phone service and quality should be comparable to WiFi. Then those GSM (GPRS) modems that connect to the USB port of your Internet device should truly be competitive with ADSL high-speed Internet. As with cellphones if you're going to be around a while, it might be worth it to buy a local SIM for your GSM modem.

Security: Rip-offs, Scams and Insurance

Of course you need to be careful at all times when traveling. You're especially vulnerable when walking around with a full pack. Don't waste time in that situation; don't do it after dark; and don't even think about it in Jo'burg, or anywhere in South Africa, for that matter. And spread that money around, on your body, that is. Don't keep everything in one easy place. Losing a little is much better than losing a lot. Got a passport bag? Don't dangle it off your neck, either inside or out. Put your arm through it and conceal it snugly under your armpit, ready to be locked down tightly, with your arm. Carry that daypack in front or off your side; a thief in a group following you closely behind can riddle through your bag without you even knowing it. Be careful with strangers;

maintain some distance. If anyone gets too close, or follows behind for too long, then stop! Let him pass.

Put that wallet in your front pocket; butts aren't so sensitive usually. Avoid crowds in general; but if you're in a crowd and feel a bump, then grab your bag or wallet immediately. You might feel someone else's hand there. That's how pickpockets work. Don't confront them; they're fast. You won't even be sure who it was. Tight passages are the same. Pickpockets wait there to pass through at the same time as you. Deal is: when you feel the bump, you won't feel the grab. If you're walking around after dark, consider carrying something gnarly in your hand, like an umbrella or a flashlight or a nasty-looking set of keys. A belt with heavy buckle that slides right out of the loops fast works well. Most thieves want to work quickly, but not all. There are slow scams and false fawning fraudulent friends, too. Remember to wear protection.

This is all for deterrence, remember; you never want to ever actually get into a tangle. If someone acts menacingly toward you and they're not yet close, then run like Hell. If they pull a gun or knife, then give them whatever they want. Your life is worth more than your iPad. In the unfortunate event that you do get robbed or mugged, don't panic. Go to the police, get a report, and start the work of canceling credit cards and getting a new passport. That means going to the nearest consulate or embassy and telling them you need an emergency termporary passport. They can usually do it in a few hours. If they imply otherwise, then talk to someone else. It can be done; I've done it. Hopefully you've got a copy of the passport; that helps. A birth certificate also helps. Remember to allow extra time at the airport of your departure, as they'll need to fix the entry stamp that's now in your lost passport. Hopefully you've got a few bucks stashed away. That helps. Don't be shy about asking for help. Get religion; that helps.

Political security is another consideration, and for an American the most thorough update is from the site already mentioned: *http://travel.state.gov*, then divide by half and that's about right (they're more cautious than your mama). Keeping up with the news is a good idea, especially for the countries where you're going. Last decade's war zones can be great travel bargains, though, like Belfast, Belgrade, Beirut, and… give Baghdad some more time. Simply put: be careful and don't take chances. An ounce of prevention is worth a kilo of cure.

I'm not a big insurance guy, considering it in general to be a rip-off, but others have differing opinions. If you're booking a flight on a multi-line booking site, it'll be available there, sometimes on individual airlines' websites also.

Some promote it heavily to pad the bill; you might have to opt out to get it off the bill. If you're going somewhere dangerous, that ups the ante a bit, of course.

Some European countries are starting to require insurance to enter their country, or so they say, but no word yet on how that's being enforced. I've never bought any kind of insurance for Europe. Obviously some of the Eastern European countries are not up to Western standards for health, safety, and welfare so insurance is worth considering if you have special need or circumstances. Worth noting is the Caucasus region, where Russia recently invaded Georgia to help Ossetia separate recently. Abkhazia is also a breakaway province of Georgia, but no violence recently. Chechnya is definitely problematic, so probably not recommended for travel. Bosnia is fine, and all of ex-Yugoslavia, for that matter. Security situations of a criminal nature are always possible for wealthy travelers in poor countries, of course, or those with criminal gangs, so that would include much of the former USSR republics, though not likely to be much of a concern unless you're scoring drugs, or procuring prostitutes, or making too many new friends too fast. Probably of more concern is the rise of thefts in hostel dorms themselves. Make sure to secure your belongings.

Health: Vaccinations, Food and Drugs

You know the drill, right? Multiple rounds of shots wherever you go and for the tropics, don't forget the prophylaxis, right? To be honest, I've never gotten most of those shots, just the ones required by law, but it would be irresponsible of me to suggest that you do the same. Tropical areas are certainly the problem, so require extra caution, though yellow fever is usually the only shot actually required by law. If you have to get that in the US just to get a visa, then it'll set you back a cool $100-150. If you can get it on the road somewhere, then it might be as little as ten bucks. Ask at public health centers; sometimes they'll jab you right at the border, just to facilitate matters. Some vaccines seem not much better than the disease, so use your judgment. Malaria prophylaxis is easy enough if you're actually entering a malarial area, but so are mosquito nets. Don't ever have sex with locals without a condom.

If the food seems strange at first wherever you happen to be, then go slow with it, allow your bacteria some time to adapt. You should experiment, though, since some of the local delicacies are delicious. Just make sure that foods have been recently made and are best served hot. The nose knows. Ask locally about water quality, though it's usually easy enough to drink bottled water or boil tap water first to be sure.

As for recreational drugs, I've got a simple rule: nothing never no way no how; just kidding! But you should be aware of the risks. A lot of countries take simple possession of marijuana as a *very serious offense*, punishable by death, or you might wish you're dead by the end of it. I would not advise traveling with ganja anywhere in the world. That smell is hard to get out. If you just gotta' have a little smoke once in a while, then I advise you to befriend the hipsters wherever you end up, which carries its own set of risks. Better yet, why not just quit for a while? You might be amazed how much easier you catch that buzz when you get home. It's the contrast that counts. Being stoned all the time is no fun. Of course more and more countries are legalizing it, so that's good. Latin America may soon be a dope-friendly continent, what with Uruguay already legal and others considering it, most of them tolerant, Europe too. Asia is intolerant.

Unfortunately more and more Muslim countries are outlawing alcohol, so it's the same thing. Take a break; you'll enjoy it more if/when you start back. Many Muslim-lite countries are growing more fundamentalist. Your best bet there are hotels, which are often considered international zones exempt from local standards. Remember that wherever you are, especially poor countries, that as a rich (yes) foreigner, you're vulnerable, so be careful. If you've just got to get a buzz once in a while, you might consider checking out the pharmacies. Things are legal overseas that are controlled tightly in the US; be creative, and read instructions carefully. It might be a good time to fix that cough. The cough syrup overseas is excellent. Check the ingredients. It even cures coughs... sometimes.

If you've got a serious drug habit, then you really should de-tox. It doesn't go well with travel. You should be careful even when drinking with locals. Mickeys do get slipped, and so do roofies. Finish that drink before going to the head. Don't accept drinks already opened, in bars or buses or trains, whether alcohol, milk or water. It's better to offend than to get robbed. Let me be clear that I do not advocate any drug use myself (I rarely if ever even drink now) but I understand the desire, so wish to see it done responsibly. But if you think you'll stay in hostels because those sound like cool places to smoke pot, then think again. I've never—I repeat, **never**—seen so much as a joint smoked at a hostel. Alcohol, yes, that's fairly common in hostels, but not pot.

As of this writing, I know of no particular health concerns in the East European region, though extra caution is always necessary in the poorer regions—Caucasus, ex-USSR, parts of Turkey, etc. Once again, probably of more concern is right there in your hostel—bedbugs. There is an infestation of them at all levels worldwide. Check your bed carefully first before using. People drink like fish, of course, all over East Europe. The beer is good and the vodka is strong. I'd be careful about scoring dope, except in pharmacies. East Europeans go to Amsterdam and stare bug-eyed like kids in a candy store.

Cultural Considerations: Sex, Religion and Politics

Among Western or westernized countries it's no big deal, of course. Our informality is our calling card and our stock in trade. That's not true elsewhere, though it's tricky to intuit. Some of the rockingest whoringest countries can be quite conservative amongst locals, Thailand for instance. In Thailand you'll rarely see locals kissing in public, though in the international zone, you'll see much more than that, of course. Vietnam has no such taboo, and couples hang all over each other in parks. Act conservatively until you know the local mores. As corny as it sounds, we are ambassadors to the world, and I'd like to think we have a larger mission to bring people together through our highest common denominators.

Think hard before taking on a local girlfriend, a good girl, that is. It'll take some time and patience. Women won't have such a problem, but just be warned that many local guys will only want a quick fling with a wild Western woman. If and when it comes time to do the nasty, always keep a few millimeters between you and the object of your affection. Anything else would be the ultimate in foolishness. Politics is always a bit dicey to discuss in public unless you know your host and his or her inclinations. Some places there can even be legal repercussions, such as Communist countries and a few Muslim ones. Tone it down. Most cultural considerations usually boil down to something much more mundane, though. Shoes are customarily removed when entering houses, and sometimes buildings, in much of the world, whether Buddhist, Hindu, or Muslim, so please comply willingly. They take it seriously.

In Eastern Europe, there are a few Muslim countries where you need to be conscious of customs—Turkey, Bosnia, Azerbaijan, Albania and Kosovo. These are mostly "Muslim Lite," so there's not much more required than taking off your shoes when entering a home, but also you should dress modestly and avoid public displays of affection. In countries where absolute freedom is less enshrined than the West, you probably want to be careful where you take pictures. I was almost hauled off to jail once by taking pictures of police lifting a drunk into a pickup truck. In many East European countries—Balkan ones, especially—people still smoke tobacco like chimneys, so that's a consideration if you're sensitive to it. I wouldn't advise lecturing the locals about it, either. Pick a hostel that's smoke-free.

What to Pack: Clothes, Communications and Cosmetics

There's one simple rule: travel light. I personally carry a day-pack and a laptop computer bag only, no matter the destination, no matter the length of the trip. Forget the monopoly board; forget the five-pound toilet kit; and most of all: forget the library (including all those 500-page travel guides), except for this book, of course. A laptop or Nook or Kindle can hold all the books you'll ever need *or you can buy whatever you need whenever you need it.* That is true of almost everything. A few changes of clothing are all you need, and a change of shoes, preferably a variety of things that can be layered as needed. The trick is to wash clothes as you go along, every chance you get, very easy if you have a private room with sink, not so easy in a dorm, but they frequently have machines there, so do everything up whenever you get the chance, except the set you're wearing.

Wear those hiking boots when you actually travel, so you never have to pack them. Add a pair of flipflops or kung fu slippers or sneakers to that, and you're set. My secret item is a down padded vest, which will compress to almost nothing, and keep you very warm in the coldest situations (plus cushion your pack and be a bus pillow and...). Add a long-sleeve shirt, and a T-shirt or two, which can go under or alone, a couple flowery shirts to accompany those pheromones you'll be sending to the opposite sex, a pair of long pants, a pair of shorts and a pair for swimming, and you're set. Use small 100ml bottles for toiletries (per carry-on restrictions), a needle and thread, a small umbrella, a power adaptor for multiple countries (and dorm rooms with few sockets), a luggage lock, and... That's about it. Don't forget the Internet device.

Eastern Europe shouldn't pose too much of a problem, except maybe in Russia or Belarus where supermarkets are still a novelty. It can get cold there, or course, some of the coldest temps on the continent right there. I can't say too much about the warmth of down and its compressibility into a small pack. Don't forget power adaptors. English-language books may be hard to find.

Travel Guides: Books, Maps and Internet

Guidebooks and internet should work together for travel, but I think the relative importance is reversed. Instead of carrying a big book around for your basic travel information and then using Internet to book hostels and play around on FaceBook, I suggest using Internet for basic travel information, too. Not only is the amount of information enormous, but it's updated constantly. This book can help finding hostels, too, whether you have Internet or not. For me large travel guides are not only an anachronism, but were never really necessary in the first place, maybe to read up on beforehand, but not to travel with. I've rarely traveled with one. Most travel is largely intuitive, and a book removes you from that. I would recommend it only in the most remote or linguistically-challenging places, when it might really aid survival.

One thing I DO like to travel with are maps. But they're cumbersome, hard to find and harder to handle. Once again Internet is perfect for this, every place in the world available from multiple views. The Internet links I've provided here all contain maps within their sites, though a simple Google search is easy enough. I look at maps the way some people look at pornography; I can't get enough of them. One of the main problems with hostels, of course, is that they're hard to find, so that you almost need detailed destructions at some point regardless. I'm hoping that this guide can help bring hostels into the mainstream and promote some standardization. There will always be local and regional quirks as to how they operate. This is a book to carry with you.

How Hostels Work

But for a few small differences, a hostel works the same as any hotel, guesthouse, lodge, B&B, whatever. I won't insult your intelligence by explaining to you that basically you're paying for a place to sleep. Where it differs mostly from the others is that at a hostel you'll likely be sharing your room with a bunch of others in similar bunk beds. That creates a unique set of circumstances which requires some attention to detail. First there's the booking process. If you're staying in a dorm, then often you'll have to decide how many roommates you want. The more roommates you have, the less the price generally.

Hostels are generally booked in advance; otherwise they can be hard to find. That's once reason this book exists, to help with last-minute walk-ups and walk-ins. That's very possible in much of Europe where hostels are properly signed and conveniently located. Call first if it's a long walk or ride. I never made an advance room reservation in twenty-five years. It's nice to be spontaneous. This way you can look at it first, too, never a bad idea if you've got the time. Don't do that around midnight. Advance booking might still be cheaper, and hostel-booking sites may be cheaper than the hostel's own website. Shop and compare. If you book in advance you'll probably need to pay a deposit in advance by credit or debit card, usually 10%. Upon arrival, you'll need to pay the rest. I'll try to tell you here which take plastic, but don't count on it. Carry enough cash, just in case. If you want extra days, advise in advance if possible. For a long stay, you might want to book two or three places two or three days at the time if you don't know them well. That way, if you get a bad one, then you'll be out soon.

Obviously there is an inherent security situation with hostels that needs addressing and some malcontents seem to have figured out the basic equation faster than those in charge. I mean… I hate to be a spoilsport, here, but just because somebody stays in a hostel doesn't mean he's honest and loyal. I don't know about you, but that's my life there in that backpack, and I'm hesitant to just toss it there on the floor and walk out assuming it's secure. That's why every hostel needs lockers, and you need a lock. Lockers don't always have them, and if there are no lockers, then try to lock your pack directly to the metal frame of the bed or something similar. No thief wants to jimmy a lock if he doesn't have to; he'll take what's easiest. If you're in the room with others, don't show a lot of valuables; the walls have eyes.

Curfews are largely a thing of the past, except in the original "youth hostels," but beware the mid-day lockout, which some places impose "for cleaning," though you and I both know they're just saving on employee costs, maybe the entire profit margin at a small place. There's a good side to that, of course: the place is secure while you're out. Conversely, since the demise of the curfew, hostels have become popular places to party, sometimes facilitated by the hostel management themselves (beware in Calgary, or Tallinn, or London, or...). If the kitchen is full of liquor bottles, then that's a good sign. If there are hordes of Homies, i.e.local non-travelers, hanging out, then that's another. The yobs coming in to London from Hounslow for the weekend tend to look and act differently than the travelers from the Continent. Another sure sign is when a hostel has its own in-house bar. I'll try to tell you here when that's the case, but read the signs at check-in also.

As already mentioned, if it's a real hostel, it should have a kitchen for your use. That's nice, especially if there are no eateries nearby. Breakfast is less important, for me at least, though coffee and tea are certainly nice. So first thing I do upon arrival is stock up on food. If you wait too long, then there's no need. I tend to carry a few basics with me, so that's a start. Having a fridge is the most important thing. It's best to keep all your things in one bag and date and mark it as yours. Check the freebies bin if you're short of something. Don't take other people's food. Ask first. Most hostel people really ARE nice.

How This Book Works

How this book works is really simple. I've given you names, addresses, and phone numbers, everything but latitude and longitude, of the hostels included, so all you have to do is find the place. I advise to call ahead if you have no reservation. And I still advise booking ahead when possible, even when it's just two or three days away, so I've included website URL's, too. Many of those have contact forms within them. I've included e-mail addresses elsewhere. If you go from hostel to hostel, then you'll usually have Internet. Where this book comes in really handy is when that link is broken and you need to find a hostel when Internet is not readily available. Invariably somewhere the Internet will be down.

Of course it's the options that constitute the decision-making process in choosing a hostel, so in this guide all are listed for the following: Kitchen (or not), Breakfast (free or not or for purchase only), Wi-Fi (free or not or for purchase only), Private rooms (available or not), Lockers (available or not), and office hours. Most of this is common sense and easily understood, but a few categories may require explanation, e.g. private rooms. Hostels may be defined by their dorm beds, but for some of us, that's not optimal. I'm a light sleeper and don't appreciate being awoken in the middle of the night. Frequently I'll pay up to double to have my own room, and even then will usually come out ahead of a hotel. Nevertheless a place that has no dorms is not a hostel in my dictionary, so it's good to have both. But if you book a private room at a hostel, don't expect the same quality as a five-star hotel, or even a one-star. It's basic, but it's yours. And you might have to pay a pretty penny for that Wi-Fi elsewhere in Europe.

Lockers are fairly rare, actually, especially considering the security risk in an open dorm. Go figure. Thefts are rising. Costs are for comparison only and are something of an average, a price actually offered at a non-peak/non-slow time of year. There are always promotions and seasonal changes and varying specifications, so check around. A hostel-booking site might be cheaper than the hostel's own site. Some hostels have free WiFi; some charge; some have none, same with computers. Contact the hostel directly if the information here is insufficient. If you don't like using a credit card online, then contact the hostel and see if other arrangements are possible. Some require full payment in advance during special seasons. There are many hostel chains now, and I may not list them all in the same town. Check their website. Most of these hostels have websites or I won't list them. Information here can be wrong. Check their website.

This book is intentionally intended to be part of a paradigm shift toward a new era in budget travel. If the old paradigm of the backpacker walking down the street with huge guidebook in hand trying to find budget accommodation is already out-of-date, then I think the one of booking them all in advance is not much better. There needs to be a balance of advance planning and spontaneity, guidebook and Internet. That's already the case, of course; I only propose to shift the balance toward less book and more Internet. This book is designed for that purpose. Not only do I hope to make hostelling better for backpackers, but I hope to see more hostels enter the mainstream, with better signage, better facilities, and ultimately more customers.

You might notice that addresses and phone numbers, everthing but Internet addresses, are listed in several different ways. That's both accidental and intentional, accidental in that I tend to leave them as they're given to me, intentional in that you'll see them many ways, so this prepares you to adapt. With phone numbers generally "+" precedes an international number. With a cell phone, hold the "0" down and "+" will appear. That saves you from having to know codes *for international calling* (011, 001, etc.) in every country. That same number used within the country would usually drop the "+" and the 2-3 number code following it and add a "0" at the front. Compare them and you'll see. A picture is worth a thousand words. Skype will add the country code for you. I sometimes use a two-digit variation of the 24-hour clock. For numbers larger than 12, subtract 12 for p.m. times. Now don't get all worried; go have some fun! Europe is at your fingertips!

Key to Symbols: Here are some symbols, shorthand and abbreviations used in this book:

–$bed = lowest price for a dorm bed that we can find for a typical day, for comparison only (they change with the season, with promotions, and with currency fluctuations)

–B'fast = Breakfast (free or not or for purchase only); typical for Europe is a "continental breakfast," pastry & drink, cereal if you're lucky; don't expect eggs; cig optional

–c.c. = credit card, OK meaning they're accepted, +/% indicating a surcharge for use; sometimes they are required as deposit, even if you're paying cash

–Recep = times when there should be someone to check you in. Don't press your luck.

–24/7 = they never close, supposedly. I suggest advising & confirming late arrival.

–HI, YHA, etc. = these are organizations of hostels which usually require membership; usually you can pay a small fee and gradually obtain membership

–central = hostel is centrally located in the city, generally a good thing for sight-seeing

–cash only = even if you reserved with plastic, they want cash for the balance

–luggage room, luggage OK, etc=you can stash your luggage to pick up later, very handy

–Y.H. = Youth Hostel

–lift = elevator

–CBD = Central Business District = city center = 'downtown'

(note: you will also see a mini-UK flag on websites to indicate English language)

Eastern Europe

In my lifetime East Europe is best known perhaps for the communism that prevailed there from WWII until 1989 and for some twenty years before WWII in Russia and the USSR. Turkey was never communist, of course, but it's arguably not even European anyway, not fully at least, Muslim in fact. And like Islam before it (and after), Communism too united various nationalities in something larger than petty nationalism, to varying degrees of success. Finally around 1989-91 the Communist "domino theory" took on new meaning and one by one, the house of cards collapsed in on itself, something which amazes me to this day. I guess you had to be there. Today East Europe is probably best defined as Slavic Europe—north and south—though there are exceptions, as already noted. Russia still leads the pack, though its growl is much whinier than before, and it has yet to lead by example. Turkey may yet regain some of its former Ottoman imperial glory if it can prove to be a Muslim leader in a confusing Arab-spring world.

1) Albania

Albania is truly the oddball nation of the Balkans. Likely descendants of the ancient Illyrians who shared the European outback with the Celts prior to the arrival of Germanic tribes, still they fared little better until united under the Ottoman banner. By adopting Islam as their religion, they were given a privileged position in the empire, and also consolidated something of a homeland for themselves, theretofore poorly defined. Annexed by the Italian fascists then the Nazis during WWII, they became Communist afterwards, with one of the most closed paranoid states to have ever existed (compare to North Korea in 2012). Much of the Islamic culture was destroyed. That ended in 1991, and Albania quickly got a rude brush with capitalism in massive Ponzi schemes that made international news in 1997. The Kosovo war (Kosovans are ethnic Albanians) also brought many refugees and ensuing problems. Things are better now and Alabania is open for business and tourism. Albanian is the language, but if you can't find someone to speak English, then try Italian. Lek (ALL) is the currency; phone code is +355.

you.travel/Albania

BERAT, like Tirana, is somewhat centrally located, and small at less than 80,000 people. Following the Greeks, Romans, Byzantines and Bulgarians, the Ottomans made Berat an important city and ultimately a center of Albanian national revival. Crafts guilds were many and varied. Today it is known for the architecture of its historic center, earning it a world heritage designation.

www.virtualtourist.com/travel/Europe/Albania/Rrethi_i_Beratit/Berat-736458/

Berat Backpackers, 295 Gorica, Berat, Albania; *beratbackpackers.com* T:693064429; *info@beratbackpackers.com;* $13bed, Kitchen:Y, B'fast:Y, WiFi:Y, Pvt.room:N, Locker:N, Recep:24/7;
Note: wheelchairs ok, bar, lounge, parking, luggage room, TV

SARANDA is on the Albanian "Riviera," directly across from the Greek Island of Corfu. There is a ferry. Nearby is the ancient city of Butrint, a world heritage site.
www.world66.com/europe/albania/saranda

Backpackers Sr-The Bunker, Rruga Mithat Hoxha #10, Lagja 4 Saranda; *www.backpackerssr.hostel.com,* T:+355694345426; $13bed, Kitchen:Y, B'fast:Y, WiFi:Y, Pvt. room:N, Locker:N, Recep:24/7;
Note: near Corfu ferry, free tour/info, luggage ok, laundry, forex, c.c. ok

Hairy Lemon, Coastal Road, Saranda; *www.hairylemonhostel.com,* T:+355693559317, *saranda@hairylemonhostel.com;* $14bed, Kitchen:Y, B'fast:Y, WiFi:Y, Pvt. room:Y, Locker:Y, Recep:24/7;
Note: lift, luggage ok, laundry, free tour, forex, prkng, not central, view

TIRANA, and Albania in general, is nothing if not chaotic and prone to extremes. Upon becoming Communist, the previous Turkish and Italian architecture was demolished or abandoned in favor of gray Bolshevik modern Stalinist style—yuk. After that, capitalism brought disorder and irregularity to an ill-prepared city. This ultimately led to great population migrations toward the countryside such that it's hard to tell where the city ends and pasture begins. It's nothing to see a five-storey building sitting out in the middle of a field, and I bet you could find cows grazing in the city if you looked hard enough. Still Tirana has its pleasures, and the cafes and bars are active. There are castles, a historic bridge, mosques, mosaics and museums. Skanderberg Square lies more or less at the center of it all. It's a mess, but really not a bad one.
www.tirana.gen.al/

Hostel-Albania, rr. Beqir Luga 56, Tirana, Albania; *www.hostel-albania.com,* T:0672783798, *Lira@Hostel-Albania.com;*

$16bed, Kitchen:Y, B'fast:Y, WiFi:Y, Pvt. room:N, Locker:Y, Recep:ltd; Note: prkng, forex, laundry, left luggage, travel info, garden, kittens! cats?

Freddy's Hostel, Ground Floor, 75 Bardhok Biba St, Tirana; *www.freddyshostel.com/*, T:(0)6820 35261; $16bed, Kitchen:N, B'fast:Y, WiFi:Y, Pvt. room:Y, Locker:N, Recep:24/7; Note: luggage room, a/c, central but hard to find

Oresti Hostel, Ground Floor 75 Bardhok Biba St, Tirana, Albania; *orestihostel.com/*, T:(0)682022313; $19bed, Kitchen:N, B'fast:N, WiFi:Y, Pvt. room:Y, Locker:N, Recep:24/7; Note: parking, forex, luggage room, a/c, non-party, ext. of Freddy's

Baron Hotel, Rruga e Elbasanit, Tirana, Albania; *www.hotelbaron.al*, T:+355682080818, *florian.kuka@hotelbaron.al*; $19bed, Kitchen:N, B'fast:Y, WiFi:Y, Pvt. room:Y, Locker:N, Recep:ltd; Note: resto/bar, laundry, luggage room, a/c, c.c. ok, in suburbs

2) Armenia

Armenia is one of three internationally-recognized nations that form the mountainous Caucasus region that for millennia has stood at the crossroads of world history. This is the bottleneck where Europe meets Asia meets the Mideast. Armenia itself begins around Mt. Ararat (Urartu) with the people we now call Urartians, an area now just inside the Turkish border. Armenia reached its greatest extent shortly before the beginning of the modern era, occupying most of the Caucasus region in addition to most of the eastern Anatolian peninsula and Syria. It was the first nation to accept Christianity as its religion. It was subsequently controlled by Byzantines and Seljuk Turks before being overrun by Mongols and soon after incorporated into the Ottoman Empire.

Turkish rule came to a sordid end with the Armenian genocide of 1915-16 at the hands of the Young Turks, an occurrence which has yet to be acknowledged by subsequent Turkish governments. The independent nation of Armenia based in Yerevan today was once a Soviet Socialist Republic and the first non-Baltic state to achieve independence. A war was fought immediately over the status of the Armenian enclave of Nogorno-Karabakh within the borders of Azerbaijan. This is a tourist goldmine, waiting to happen. I hope you like vodka. You don't speak Armenian? No problem. Almost everyone still speaks Russian, too. *Dram* (AMD) is the currency; calling code is +374.

www.welcomearmenia.com/

YEREVAN is the capital of modern Armenia and can trace its history back to 782 BC as Yerebuni, making it among Europe's oldest. Sitting smack on the crossroads of space and time will put you through some changes, of course, and Yerevan has seen it all (or most of it, anyway) with Arabs, Persians, Ottomans, and Russians all leaving their tracks on Yerevan's face.

Things were hard after independence, too, but are gradually getting better, with construction booming and the bars and clubs full. They've even got bars in the parks, complete with sofas! How's that for service? Still the symbol of Armenia, Mt. Ararat of Noah's Ark fame, sits there in the distance, visible from any angle, across the border in Turkey. Ouch! That's gotta' hurt. Armenians love to party; did I mention?
armeniapedia.org/index.php?title=Yerevan

Envoy Hostel, 54 Pushkin St, Yerevan, Armenia;
www.envoyhostel.com, T:(8)10530369, *info@envoyhostel.com*; $17bed,
Kitchen:Y, B'fast:Y, WiFi:Y, Pvt. room:Y, Locker:Y, Recep:24/7;
Note: laundry, luggage room, free tour, parking, TV, a/c, c.c. ok, central

Penthouse Hostel & Hotel, Koryun 5, Yerevan, Armenia;
www.penthousehostel.org/, T:+37477028913, *info@penthousehostel.org*;
$12bed, Kitchen:Y, B'fast:Y, WiFi:Y, Pvt. room:Y, Locker:N, Recep:24/7;
Note: bar, laundry, luggage room, a/c

Yerevan Hostel, Tpagrichneri 5, Yerevan, Armenia;
http://hostelinyerevan.com/, T:+37410547757; $14bed,
Kitchen:Y, B'fast:Y, WiFi:Y, Pvt. room:Y, Locker:Y, Recep:24/7;
Note: bar, parking, luggage room, laundry, forex, a/c, c.c. ok, central

Theatre Hostel, 27 Tigran Metz Ave, 2nd Entrance, Yerevan;
www.theatre.am, T:(8)10545676, *info@theatre.am*; $11bed,
Kitchen:Y, B'fast:Y, WiFi:Y, Pvt. room:Y, Locker:N, Recep:ltd;
Note: free tour/info, laundry, luggage ok, a/c, c.c., midday lockout

3) Azerbaijan

Azerbaijan is the largest in size but least of the Caucasian republics in many ways—least visited, least known, least understood. What's there is impressive. It is the first democratic secular majority-Muslim republic. It is one of six Turkic republics, and the one that links modern Turkey with its relatives back east—Turkmenistan, Uzbekistan, Kyrgyzstan, and Kazakhstan. It lost Nagorno-Karabakh to the local Armenians and has an enclave in Naxchivan totally detached from the rest of the country. Legendary Scythians from the far eastern steppes were among the area's earliest inhabitants and then came Alexander's Greeks, but like all the Turkic republics, conflict between local Turks and ethnic Iranians supply most of the political drama throughout history. Turks have been dominant for the last millennium, though, often sharing territory with Armenians, Russians, and others.

Azerbaijan is not defined by politics or religion, however, so much as its signature natural resource, one which many countries would die for—oil. Oil has been traded here since the earliest centuries of the modern era, and is making a strong comeback with the rise in prices. There are rich folk traditions in music, dance, and textiles, as well as more modern accomplishments in literature, architecture, and cinema. The petroglyphs at Gobustan are a UNESCO world heritage site. Azerbaijani is the language; *manat* (AZN) is currency; phone code is +994.

www.azerbaijan.com/

BAKU is the home of Azerbaijan's oil industry and a century ago produced as much as one-half of the world's oil, though full-scale production long predates that. Today it is home to one-fourth of all Azeris and until recently was a cosmopolitan city of many ethnicities. The break with Russia and war

in Nagorno-Karabakh changed all that. Still it is a secular city and there is plenty of nightlife and entertainment, including a thriving music scene. And like many oil towns, it's not cheap. The walled city is a UNESCO world heritage site, a maze of narrow alleys and ancient buildings. In it are the 12th C. Maiden's Tower, the 11th C. Palace of the Shīrvān-Shāhs, the Synyk-Kala Minaret and Mosque, the law court (Divan-Khan), the Dzhuma-Mechet Minaret, and the mausoleum of the astronomer Seida Bakuvi. There are several museums, too.
www.azerbaijan24.com/

Caspian Hostel, Asəf Zeynallı, Küçəsi 29/10 İçəri Şəhər, Bakı; *seyf@box.az*; T:+994(0)124921995; $22bed, Kitchen:Y, B'fast:N, WiFi:Y, Pvt. room:N, Locker:N, Recep:24/7; Note: old town, a/c, luggage ok, pool, TV, parking

4) Belarus

Belarus is the country variously referred to historically as Byelorussia, "White Russia" and so forth, and emerged in the same phenomenon that included Kievan Rus, the act of Varangians catalyzing local Slavs into political entities. The Mongol hordes destroyed all that, of course, but the culture reemerged intact and has been paired variously with neighbors Poland, Lithuania, and most of all Russia. That is the case in post-communist Europe, where Belarus has the reputation as least-changed of all the ex-USSR constituent states, due mostly to the autocratic rule of Alexander Lukashenko. That in itself is tour-worthy, I suppose, but it might cost as much money and hassle as Russia, for a country much smaller. There are four world heritage sites, though, and it's on my list. A transit visa might work, three days to cross from Ukraine via Belarus to Lithuania or vice-versa sounds about right; train from Warsaw via Belarus to Moscow would also work. Belarusian *ruble* (BYR) is currency; Belarusian and Russian are the languages; calling code is +375.

www.belarus.by/en/

MINSK is the capital and largest city of Belarus. It is also headquarters for the CIS, the union of ex-USSR members. It is documented from the 11th century and was a part of the Grand Duchy of Lithuania as well as the Polish-Lithuanian commonwealth. It was annexed by Russia in 1793 and became a Soviet Socialist Republic in the USSR. Minsk was always a center for foreigners, but WWII decimated the Jewish population and Soviet policies afterwards didn't help, so many have since left. Polish people still have a presence here. The major foreign presence is Russian, though, as Belarus still has a political relationship with Russia, and may in fact never totally break away. Tourism is in its infancy. There are many churches and cathedrals, but the main attraction is the general atmosphere of fear and paranoia.

www.inyourpocket.com/belarus/minsk

Hostel Jazz, Mosirskaya St 37A, Minsk, Belarus; *http://hosteljazz.by*, T:+375(8)333361633, *hostel.jazz@gmail.com*; $10bed, Kitchen:Y, B'fast:N, WiFi:Y, Pvt. room:Y, Locker:N, Recep:24/7;
Note: bike rent, pool, tour desk, luggage room, TV

Hostel Postoyalets, Partizansky Ave. 147, Minsk, Belarus; *postoyalets.by/*, T:(8)172434981, *res@postoyalets.by*; $14bed, Kitchen:Y, B'fast:N, WiFi:Y, Pvt. room:N, Locker:N, Recep:24/7;
Note: central, TV, pool, luggage room

5) Bosnia & Hercegovina

If the Balkans (mostly ex-Yugoslavia) consists primarily of a single ethnic group and language family, i.e. southern Slavic, it certainly consists of at least three culturally different "constituent peoples," all of them present in modern Bosnia—Serbs with their orthodox Christian church and Cyrillic script, Croats with their Catholic church and Roman script, and lastly Bosniaks, with their Islam (to use Arabic script would be almost too perfect). In an area previously settled by Illyrians and Celts, Slavs came to settle in the last half of the first millennium AD, and eventually established a political entity which became the Kingdom of Bosnia. It was long-lasting, but not stable, however, and the Ottoman Turks finally annexed it in 1463 and ruled for more than four centuries. These Slavs were last to convert to Christianity, which may have made them more convertible to Islam by the Ottoman Turks. Whatever, it worked, of course, and Bosnia to this day has almost more vestiges of Turkish culture, including *kilims* and cuisine, than does much of Turkey itself.

By the 19th century Ottoman Turkey was in serious decline, and Austria-Hungary assumed control in 1879. Germany and Russia signed off on it, but not Serbia, and all bets were off when a Serb nationalist in the Bosnian capital of Sarajevo killed the Austrian archduke and started WWI. After the war Bosnia joined the nascent Yugoslavia, though Bosnian Muslims were not well-represented in the political mix, and internal boundaries were redrawn to minimize their influence. WWII was horrific, with Serbian-nationalist Chetniks no better than the Nazis, but Bosnia remained as one of six constituent republics in the post-war Communist government and it prospered as a center of the defense industry. Post-Communist independence finally came in 1991.

Unfortunately it is politically divided between Serb-dominated *Republika Srpski* on one hand, and a union of Croats and Bosniaks on the other, and that's the good news. The bad news is that the Muslims endured a Serb-sponsored genocide/ethnic cleansing from 1992-95 in the process. The rest is silence. None of Bosnia's horror is a reason to avoid tourism here, quite the contrary in fact. The famous city of Sarajevo is here and so is the historic city of Mostar. The countryside is beautiful and underpopulated. The food is good. The currency is the convertible Mark (BAM); the language is Bosnian (Serbo-Croatian); the calling code is +387.

www.tourism-in-bosnia.com/

BANJALUKA is the main city of the Republika Srpska region of Bosnia and site of many uprisings against the Ottoman overlords in the 19th century. In 1993 Bosnian Serbs destroyed two large historic mosques in the city dating from the Ottoman period, the Ferhadija and the Arnaudija mosques. This is the center from which Croats and Bosnians were raped and massacred in the name of "ethnic cleansing" during the Bosnian War of 1992-95. There is a concentration camp. I just report the facts. You do what you want. Flowers would be nice.

www.bhtourism.ba/eng/banjaluka.wbsp

City Smile Hostel, Skendera Kulenovića 16, Banjaluka, Rep. Serbski; *www.hostel-banjaluka.com*, T:+38751214187; $15bed, Kitchen:Y, B'fast:N, WiFi:Y, Pvt. room:Y, Locker:Y, Recep:24/7;
Note: coffee & tea, parking, luggage room

MOSTAR is the main city in the Hercegovina part of B & H. It was named after the keepers of its most famous landmark, the old bridge (*stari most*), built by the Ottomans and spanning the Neretva River. Halfway between Sarajevo and the sea, this has been a trade route and river crossing since antiquity. The city as we know it was constructed by the Turks in their fashion, and, after recent years as part of Austria-Hungary, Yugoslavia, and then the Serbian siege, it has been reconstructed in that fashion. If you want to see how Ottoman Turkey used to be, then go to Mostar. There are Greek and Roman ruins, too. The bridge is a World Heritage site. Islam is the religion here, so be prepared to take your shoes off when going inside (and please don't bitch about it; it's impolite).

www.visitmostar.net/

Guest House Taso, M.TITA 187, Mostar, Bosnia-Herzegovina; *www.guesthousetaso.com*, T:061523149, *guesthousetaso@gmail.com;* $14bed, Kitchen:Y, B'fast:N, WiFi:Y, Pvt. room:Y, Locker:N, Recep:24/7;
Note: free pick-ups, club, parking, travel desk, age limit 45 y.o.

Hostel Majdas, Franje Milicevica 39, Mostar, Bosnia-Herzegovina; *www.hostelmajdas.com/*, T:+38761382940, *majdasofra@yahoo.com;* $17bed, Kitchen:Y, B'fast:Y, WiFi:Y, Pvt. room:N, Locker:Y, Recep:>10p;
Note: free pickups, age limit 45, luggage room, laundry, forex, parking, a/c

Rooms Denino, Trg Ivana Krndelja 11F, Mostar, Bosnia-Herzegovina; *sobe-denino.com*, T:+38736550372, *maida_begic@yahoo.com;* $15bed, Kitchen:N, B'fast:$, WiFi:N, Pvt. room:Y, Locker:Y, Recep:24/7;
Note: resto/bar, pick-ups, luggage room, laundry, forex, central, Mama M

Hostel Miran, Pere Lažetića 13 (Carina), Mostar, Bosnia-Hercegovina; *www.hostelmiran-mostar.com*, T:061823555, *meskic_mo@hotmail.com;* $13bed, Kitchen:Y, B'fast:$, WiFi:N, Pvt. room:Y, Locker:N, Recep:24/7;
Note: laundry, luggage room, forex, free tour, travel desk, family-run

Hostel Miturno, Brace Fejica 67, Mostar, Bosnia-Hercegovina; *www.hostel-miturno.ba/*, T:+38736552408, *bookings@miturno.ba;* $13bed, Kitchen:Y, B'fast:$, WiFi:Y, Pvt. room:Y, Locker:N, Recep:24/7;
Note: bar, laundry, luggage room, a/c, c.c. ok, forex, central

Hostel Dino, Mladena Balorde 1 (Musala Square), Mostar, B & H; *www.hostel-dino.hostel.com/*, T:061968119, *dino.hostel@gmail.com;* $13bed, Kitchen:N, B'fast:$, WiFi:Y, Pvt. room:Y, Locker:Y, Recep:24/7;
Note: free pick-up, prkng, laundry, luggage room, a/c, central, near bus

SARAJEVO is the capital of B & H, high up in the Dinaric Alps, and is a world city in every sense, until recently having adherents of four major religions within its environs, and having once hosted the Winter Olympics. During the Ottoman era it was constructed largely in Turkish style and had many times the population of any other Balkan city. Eventually it was annexed by Austria-Hungary and WWI started right here when Archduke Franz Ferdinand was assassinated by a Serb nationalist. In the War of Independence following the breakup of Yugoslavia, Sarajevo was besieged and blockaded by Serb forces from 1992-5, resulting in tens of thousands of casualties and much physical damage.

Today Sarajevo prospers again and is one of the fastest-growing cities in the region. It has film and jazz festivals, a music subculture, and was one of the highlights of my "Hypertravel" project. Principal mosques and Islamic structures are the Gazi Husreff-Bey's Mosque, the Mosque of Ali Pasha, the *medrese* (madrasah), the Imaret (a free kitchen for the poor), the *hamam* (public baths), and a late 16th-century clock tower. Museums include the Mlada Bosna, the Museum of the Revolution, and a Jewish museum. Did I mention that it's a travel bargain? Hostel quality is good. Many buildings are still riddled, by bullets, not mysteries. But wait...

www.sarajevo-tourism.com

Travellers' Home, Ćumurija 4, Sarajevo, Bosnia and Herzegovina; *www.myhostel.ba/*, T:(0)70242400, *info@myhostel.ba*; $16bed, Kitchen:Y, B'fast:Y, WiFi:Y, Pvt. room:Y, Locker:Y, Recep:24/7; Note: café, parking, tour, travel desk, laundry, luggage room

Residence Rooms, s.h.Muvekita 1, Sarajevo, Bosnia-Herzegovina; *www.residencerooms.com.ba*, T:066801727, *residencerooms@gmail.com*; $16bed, Kitchen:Y, B'fast:Y, WiFi:Y, Pvt.room:Y, Locker:Y, Recep:24/7; Note: café, laundry, luggage room, central, tours, outside noise

Hostel Ferhadija, Ferhadija 21, Sarajevo, *hostel-ferhadija.com.ba/*, T:070213220, *hostel.ferhadija.sarajevo@gmail.colm;* $17bed, Kitchen:Y, B'fast:N, WiFi:Y, Pvt. room:Y, Locker:Y, Recep:24/7; Note: café, luggage room, TV, a/c, central

Hostel Srce Sarajeva, S.H.Muvekita 2 71000, Sarajevo, Bosnia/Herz; *hostelsrcesarajeva.ba/*, T:033442887, *hostelsrcesarajeva@gmail.com*; $20bed, Kitchen:Y, B'fast:N, WiFi:Y, Pvt. room:Y, Locker:Y, Recep:24/7;
Note: coffee & tea, parking, laundry, free tour, a/c, c.c. ok, hard to find

Hasris Youth Hostel, Vratnik Mejdan 29, Sarajevo, Bosnia/Herzeg; *www.hyh.ba/*, T:(0)61518825, *info@hyh.ba*; $20bed, Kitchen:Y, B'fast:N, WiFi:Y, Pvt. room:Y, Locker:Y, Recep:8a>4p;
Note: bar, hubbly-bubbly, views, laundry, luggage ok, c.c. ok, uphill

Hostel City Center Sarajevo, Saliha Hadzihuseinovica, Muvekita 2/3; *www.hcc.ba/sarajevo/*, T:(0)62993330, *hcc.sarajevo@hcc.ba*; $20bed, Kitchen:Y, B'fast:Y, WiFi:Y, Pvt. room:N, Locker:Y, Recep:24/7;
Note: laundry, luggage room, free tour, travel desk, a/c, c.c. ok, stairs

B & B Divan, Mula Mustafe Baseskija 54, Sarajevo, Bosnia/Herz; *pansiondivan.ba*, T:(0)33238677, *info@pansiondivan.ba*; $20bed, Kitchen:N, B'fast:$, WiFi:$, Pvt. room:Y, Locker:Y, Recep: 24/7;
Note: laundry, travel desk, a/c, c.c. ok, central, dorm room in hotel

Pansion Lion, Bravadžiluk 30, Old Town Sarajevo, Bosnia/Herzeg; *www.lion.co.ba/*, T:(0)33236137, *lionsarajevo@gmail.com*; $29bed, Kitchen:N, B'fast:$, WiFi:N, Pvt. room:Y, Locker:N, Recep: 24/7;
Note: luggage room, laundry, a/c, central, family-run

Hostel Tito 46, Marsala tita 46, Sarajevo, Bosnia/Herzegovina; *hostel-tito46.com/*, T:+38763693275, *info@hostel-tito46.com*; $13bed, Kitchen:Y, B'fast:$, WiFi:Y, Pvt. room:Y, Locker:Y, Recep:ltd;
Note: laundry, travel desk, forex, ATM, TV, bike rent, central

Hostel Ljubcica, Mula Mustafe Baeskije 65, Bascarsija, Sarajevo, B/H, *www.hostelljubicica.net/*, T:033535829, *taljubic@bih.net.ba*; $9bed, Kitchen:N, B'fast:$, WiFi:Y, Pvt. room:N, Locker:Y, Recep:24/7;
Note: bar, laundry, luggage room, parking, central, pick-ups

6) Bulgaria

The Thracians, Greeks and Romans each once colonized the area now known as Bulgaria, before Slavs swarmed in to populate it in the 6th century. But the Bulgars ruled, they an eastern steppes tribe who adopted the Slavic language, the Bulgarian form of which is now considered one of the most "original." Such are the zigzags of history. The First Bulgarian Empire lasted for several centuries before being defeated by the Byzantines in 1018. After re-establishing their empire, five centuries of Ottoman rule came in 1393. It was not pretty, and with the help of Russia, independence finally came in 1878. A period of militarism followed, including losses in WWI & II, before the period of one-party Communist rule and rapid industrialization.

Free elections in 1990 brought a ten-year rough patch, but things are better now and Bulgaria is now a member of NATO and the EU. Tourist attractions include the ancient cities of Plovdiv and Nesebar, national parks, and the rock-hewn churches of Ivanovo. Nestinarstvo is a ritual fire dance. Bulgarian folk music is renowned. They dance; they sing; they rock; sounds good to me. The food is good, too. Bulgarian is the language; the currency is *lev* (BGN); the calling code is +359.

bulgariatravel.org/

NESSEBAR is a culture-rich city on the Black Sea coast, beginning with the Greek colony of Mesembria in the 6th century BC. Much of the world's ancient history left its mark here at one time or other. The entire town is a world heritage site. Remains include the 6th C. Old Metropolitan Church and the 12th C. New Metropolitan Church.

http://visitnessebar.org/

Guest House Edelweiss, ul.Edelweiss 5, Nessebar, Bulgaria BG-8230; *www.hostelnesebar.com*; $12bed, Kitchen:Y, B'fast:N, WiFi:Y, Pvt.room:Y, Locker:N, Recep:ltd; Note: laundry, forex, a/c, TV, in apt. block

PLOVDIV is Bulgaria's second city and is centrally located within the country. It is historically a rich agricultural region, only to become industrialized in the Communist era. In the old Trimontium quarter of the city, parts of the Roman walls remain. The medieval ruins of Tsar Ivan Asen II's fortress and Bachkovo monastery are nearby. Cultural institutions include a museum.

www.inyourpocket.com/Bulgaria/plovdiv

Plovdiv Guesthouse, 20 Saborna St., Plovdiv, Bulgaria, EU; *www.plovdivguesthouse.com*, T:032622432, *info@plovdivguest.com*; $12bed, Kitchen:Y, B'fast:Y, WiFi:$, Pvt. room:Y, Locker:N, Recep:24/7;
Note: laundry, a/c, c.c. ok, central

Hikers' Hostel, 53 Saborna St, Plovdiv, Bulgaria; *www.hikers-hostel.org*, **T:**+359885194553, *plovdiv@hikers-hostel.org*; $13bed, Kitchen:N, B'fast:$, WiFi:Y, Pvt.room:Y, Locker:N, Recep:24/7;
Note: free airport pick-up, a/c, bar, laundry, multiple locations

RUSE began its history as a Roman fortified harbor and reached the peak of its importance as a base for the Ottoman Turks. Located on the far northern border of the country, on the right bank of the Danube, it is known for its Neo-Baroque-Rococo architecture. There are also festivals, museums, and other places of cultural interest.

www.travelgrove.com/travel-guides/Bulgaria/Ruse-Map-c200243.html

Villa Slanchevo, 14 Stara Planina Street, Village of Pisanets, Ruse; *www.villaslanchevo.hostel.com/*, T:+359885447452; $13bed,

Kitchen:Y, B'fast:Y, WiFi:Y, Pvt. room:N, Locker:Y, Recep:24/7;
Note: in Pisanets, 25 kms E. of Ruse, wheelchair ok, parking, laundry

SOFIA is the capital and largest city of Bulgaria, and is located in the western part of the country. Its role as Bulgaria's main city only arose after liberation from the Ottoman Empire not even a hundred-and-fifty years ago, when the population was little over 10,000 people. After suffering huge losses during the era of the WW's, Sofia is doing better in the era of the www's. Travelers have flocked to Sofia *en masse,* it being something of a convenient crossroads between Athens, Istanbul, and Belgrade. This is the main overland backpacker route east from Budapest. Prices are good, the food is good, and the beer is cold. There are world heritage sites, green areas, and museums. Besides the restored St. George, Boyana, and St. Sofia churches, historical monuments include two mosques and the Alexander Nevsky Cathedral. There are many museums, and the city is attractive and well-proportioned. Arts and entertainment are lively.

www.4smarttourists.com/bulgaria/sofia-capital/sofia/

Canape Connection, 12A, William Gladstone St., Sofia, Bulgaria;
canapeconnection.com/, T:24416373, *hostel@canapeconnection.net;*
$15bed, Kitchen:Y, B'fast:Y, WiFi:Y, Pvt.room:Y, Locker:N,
Recep:24/7;
Note: luggage room, free tour, a/c, c.c. ok, near cafes & bars,
pancakes!

Hostel Mostel, Makedonia Blvd 2, Sofia, Bulgaria;
www.hostelmostel.com/, T:0889223296, *info@hostelmostel.com*; $13bed,
Kitchen:Y, B'fast:Y, WiFi:Y, Pvt. room:Y, Locker:Y, Recep:24/7;
Note: luggage room, parking, travel info, central, free dinner, coffee/
tea

Kervan Hostel, Sofia, Rositsa St 3, Bulgaria;
www.kervanhostel.com/, T:029839428, *kervanhostel@abv.bg;* $16bed,
Kitchen:Y, B'fast:N, WiFi:Y, Pvt. room:Y, Locker:N, Recep:24/7;
Note: tour info, safe dep., non-party, central

Nightingale Hostel, 2A, Petko R. Slaveykov Square, Sofia, Bulgaria; *www.nightingale.hostel.com/*, T:+359877214888; $12bed, Kitchen:Y, B'fast:Y, WiFi:Y, Pvt. room:Y, Locker:Y, Recep:ltd;
Note: café/bar/club, pool, luggage room, bike rent, ATM, laundry

Internet Hostel Sofia, 50A Alabin St, 2nd Fl, 6 Apt, Sofia, Bulgaria; *www.internethostelsofia.hostel.com/* T:+359889138298; $13bed, Kitchen:Y, B'fast:N, WiFi:Y, Pvt. room:Y, Locker:Y, Recep:24/7;
Note: resto-bar, luggage ok, laundry, central

Hostel Lavele, 14, Lavele St, Sofia, Bulgaria; *www.lavelehostel.com*, T:0884080283, *lavelehostel@gmail.com;* $12bed, Kitchen:N, B'fast:Y, WiFi:Y, Pvt. room:Y, Locker:Y, Recep:ltd;
Note: luggage room, laundry, tour info, c.c. ok, central, no bunks

Hostel Gulliver, Dondukov Blvd. 48, 2nd Fl, Sofia, Bulgaria; *www.hostelgulliver.com/*, T:+35929875210, *info@gulliver1947-bg.com*; $12bed, Kitchen:N, B'fast:Y, WiFi:Y, Pvt. room:Y, Locker:N, Recep:24/7;
Note: laundry, travel info, central, coffee & tea

Elysia Hostel, Pop Bogomil St. 8, Sofia, Bulgaria; *www.elysiahotel.com/*, T:(+359)897085791, *elysiahotel@gmail.com*; $15bed, Kitchen:Y, B'fast:Y, WiFi:Y, Pvt. room:Y, Locker:N, Recep:24/7;
Note: parking, luggage room, wheelchair ok, central

Art Hostel, 21/A, Angel Kanchev St, Sofia, Bulgaria; *www.art-hostel.com*, T:+35929870545, *art-hostel@art-hostel.com*; $17bed, Kitchen:Y, B'fast:Y, WiFi:Y, Pvt.room:Y, Locker:N, Recep:24/7;
Note: bar, laundry, luggage room, c.c. ok, garden

Orient Express Hostel, **8A Christo Belchev St, 3rd Fl,** Sofia, Bulgaria; *orientexpresshostel.com/*, **T:0888384828**, *orientexpresshostel@yahoo.com;* $12bed, Kitchen:Y, B'fast:Y, WiFi:Y, Pvt. room:Y, Locker:Y, Recep:24/7;

Note: bar/club, laundry, luggage ok, forex, c.c. ok, central, no lift

VARNA is Bulgaria's third city and the seaside resort. The area it occupies has been occupied since pre-history: Varna culture, then Thracians, Greeks, Romans, and Ottomans that read like a TOC to Western civilization in addition to the Slavs who live here now. These ruins are now tourist sites, too, especially ancient Roman Odessus, and the beach. The Crusades ended here, also, contemporaneous with the Ottoman Conquest. There are the 4th C. Aladzha Monastery, overlooking the city from the north and a 5th /6th C. basilica remaining from an ancient Genoese colony. Varna was once named Stalin.

www.varna.bg/en/

Hostel del Mar, 29 Kraibrejna St. Varna, Bulgaria;
www.delmarvarna.com/, T:0888384828, *hosteldelmar@yahoo.com;*
$7bed, Kitchen:Y, B'fast:Y, WiFi:Y, Pvt. room:Y, Locker:Y, Recep:24/7;
Note: parking, forex, luggage room, terrace, garden sea views, not central

Yo-Ho-Hostel, bul Russestr 23, Varna, Bulgaria;
www.yohohostel.com/, T:(+359)886382905, *hostel@yohohostel.com;*
$9bed, Kitchen:Y, B'fast:Y, WiFi:Y, Pvt. room:Y, Locker:N, Recep:24/7;
Note: bar, forex, parking, travel info, Ziggy the dog, central

VELIKO TARNOVO means "old" Tarnovo, and that defines the place, medieval and walled and the most important city in the Second Bulgarian Empire of the 12th-14th centuries. It even called itself the "Third Rome" at the time. The Ottomans crushed all that. Tarnovo gets the last laugh, though, with today almost as many tourist sites as Istanbul itself, if not Rome. Did I mention that the houses, built in terraces, appear to be stacked one atop the other? There are also the Church of the Forty Martyrs and the 14th C. Church of St. Peter and St. Paul. There are eleven monasteries, including Sveta Troitsa ("Holy Trinity"), and the town has an archaeological museum.

www.veliko.co.uk/index.php

Hostel Mostel, 10, Yordan Indjeto St, Veliko Tarnovo, Bulgaria; *www.hostelmostel.com*, T:0897859359, *getinfo@hostelmostel.com;* $12bed, Kitchen:Y, B'fast:Y, WiFi:Y, Pvt. room:Y, Locker:Y, Recep:24/7;
Note: bar, parking. laundry, luggage room, dinner

Nomads Hostel, 27 Gurko St, Veliko Tarnovo, Bulgaria; *www.nomadshostel.com*, T:+35962603092, *info@nomadshostel.com*; $12bed, Kitchen:Y, B'fast:Y, WiFi:Y, Pvt. room:N, Locker:Y, Recep:24/7;
Note: bar/club, laundry, luggage, a/c, c.c. ok, central, views

Guest House Stambolov, Ulitsa Stefan Stambolov 27, V. Tarnovo; *www.hotelstambolov.com*, T:0888835048, *stambolov27@abv.bg;* $10bed, Kitchen:N, B'fast:$, WiFi:Y, Pvt.room:Y, Locker:Y, Recep:24/7;
Note: resto/bar, laundry, luggage room, parking, a/c, c.c. ok

7) Croatia

Croatia is the most western of the three Serbo-Bosnian-Croatian countries and forms something of a pincers formation around a wedge-like Bosnia, which more-or-less represents the leading edge of Ottoman domination in the region. These southern Slavs have been in the region at least since the seventh century, gradually edging Roman settlements back toward the sea, an area under Croat control today and which until recently still spoke the Romance Dalmatian language. For the first two centuries of their existence in the area, Croats were an independent kingdom before entering a personal union with Hungary in 1102. As Venice assumed control over the Dalmatian coast and the Ottomans threatened the whole peninsula, Croatia joined the House of Habsburg as a defensive strategy in 1526, and a military frontier was created and enforced. As a result Croatia was able to stay out of Ottoman influence, while Bosnia remained within.

In the 20th century the political landscape changed: Austria-Hungary fell, and the union of Serbs, Croats and Slovenes eventually became the nascent Yugoslavia. They became Communist after WWII, of course, and independent of Russia, but not Serbia. The Croatian War of Independence in the early 1990's was brutal, but Croatia prevailed and today life is good. That Dalmatian coast is Croatia's tourist gold these days, too, with cities like Dubrovnik and Split leading the way. Hostel quality is not bad, either, though they're not very good with formalities like websites. I prefer those with them (hint hint). *Kuna* (HRK) is the currency; Croat is the language; the calling code is +385.

www.visit-croatia.co.uk/

DUBROVNIK is one of Europe's top tourist destinations for over a hundred years, its walled medieval city the main draw. As Ragusa, this was a maritime city that goes back to the Roman era, was later ruled by the Byzantines, and rivaled Venice in the Middle Ages, before becoming a colony of it. Though it later paid tribute to the Turkish Ottomans, Ragusa was a free city until the Austrian Habsburgs took over in 1815. At that point Dubrovnik was Europe in microcosm, with German, Latin, and Slavic languages all spoken within its domain. Then came Yugoslavia and Communism. After Croatia's declaration of independence in 1991, Dubrovnik was besieged by the rump Yugoslavia for seven months, Montenegro claiming that Dubrovnik belonged to it. The siege was finally lifted and damage to the old city repaired. There are 2km of walls around it.

The old city is a UNESCO World Heritage site. Landmarks include two 14th C. convents at the ends of the city, the Rector's Palace, numerous fortresses, a 16-sided fountain and bell tower, and a 15th C. Jewish synagogue. The island of Lokrum has gardens and orange groves, in addition to a fortress and monastery. Museums include the Museum of Dubrovnik, the Franciscan monastery, the Maritime Museum, and the Dubrovnik State Archives. There is a 45-day long summer festival. There are many cheap accommodations, but few have dorms. Here are some that do.

www.tzdubrovnik.hr/eng/

Fresh Sheets Hostel Dubrovnik Old Town, Svetog Šimuna 15, *www.freshsheetshostel.com/*, T:0917992086, *beds@igotfresh.com;* $39bed, Kitchen:Y, B'fast:Y, WiFi:Y, Pvt. room:Y, Locker:Y, Recep:ltd; Note: in the old city, lots of stairs

Hostel & Rooms Ana- Old Town Dubrovnik, Kovačka 4, Dubrovnik; *www.hostelanadubrovnik.hostel.com*, T:098674188; $35bed, Kitchen:Y, B'fast:N, WiFi:Y, Pvt. room:Y, Locker:N, Recep:24/7; Note: above Irish Pub, "replacement" rooms around town, lotta steps

Vila Micika, Mata Vodopica 10, Lapad, Dubrovnik, Croatia; *www.vilamicika.hr/*, T:020437332, *info@vilamicika.hr*; $34bed, Kitchen:N, B'fast:N, WiFi:Y, Pvt. room:Y, Locker:Y, Recep:24/7; Note: free bus/ferry pickup, resto/bar, supermkt, laundry, prkng, a/c

Youth Hostel Dubrovnik, Vinka Sagrestana 3, Dubrovnik, Croatia; *www.hihostels.com*, T:+38520423241, *dubrovnik@hfhs.hr*; $22bed, Kitchen:Y, B'fast:Y, WiFi:N, Pvt. room:N, Locker:N, Recep:ltd; Note: by old city, member discount, resto, luggage ok, c.c. ok, uphill

HVAR is a city and island off the Croatian coast, and over forty miles long. The old city originally founded by the Greeks is one of Europe's oldest. The city was a medieval naval base. The divided fields of Stari Grad Plain are a UNESCO world heritage site, evidence of the agricultural style of the ancient Greeks.

www.hvarinfo.com/

Villa Zorana, Domovinskog rata 20, Hvar, Croatia; *www.vilazorana.hostel.com*, T:+385917231737; $18bed, Kitchen:Y, B'fast:N, WiFi:Y, Pvt. room:Y, Locker:Y, Recep:24/7; Note: luggage ok, laundry, bikes, prkng, a/c, central, 2 Night min

Dink's Place, Ive Roića 5, Vrisak, Hvar, Croatia; *www.dinksplace.com*, T:0917866923, *info@dinksplace.com;* $25bed, Kitchen:Y, B'fast:N, WiFi:Y, Pvt. room:Y, Locker:Y, Recep:ltd; Note: luggage room, laundry, parking, forex, min. stay 2 nights

Phara Hostel, Gdinj b.b., Hvar, Croatia; *www.phara-hostel.com/*, T:021776044, *phara.hostel@gmail.com*; $26bed, Kitchen:N, B'fast:N, WiFi:Y, Pvt.room:Y, Locker:Y, Recep:>11p; Note: laundry, parking, cash only, distant so car necessary, noon lockout

KORCULA is a town and an island in the Dalmatian archipelago which also includes the other towns of Vela Luka and Blato. Ferries and catamarans connect it with other towns and islands in the region and with Italy in the summer. The old town is a well-preserved 16th C. town. Marco Polo was supposedly born here.

www.korculainfo.com/

Dragan's Den Hostel, Ulica 91, Korčula, Croatia;

www.dragansden.hostel.com/ T:0981655914; $18bed, Kitchen:Y, B'fast:N, WiFi:Y, Pvt. room:Y, Locker:N, Recep:24/7; Note: free shuttle, pool, basement dorm no window, free laundry

PULA lies at the tip of the Istrian peninsula and is the largest city in the county of the same name. It entered the pages of history with the Greeks a millennium before the Common Era and then as the *Histri* during the Roman Era. The history of rulers here is like a rollcall of Western history—Ostrogoths, Byzantines, and Charlemagne, Venice, Genoa, and Pisa. Slavs eventually outnumbered Italians and the Istrian peninsula joined Croatia and Yugoslavia in 1947. Winemaking, fishing and tourism are the major industries. Roman ruins, including an amphitheatre, and beaches top the list of tourist destinations.

www.pulainfo.hr/en/

Pula Art Hostel, Maruliceva 41, Pula, Croatia; *www.pulaarthostel.com*, T:+38598874078, *booking@pulaarthostel.com*; $19bed, Kitchen:Y, B'fast:N, WiFi:Y, Pvt. room:N, Locker:Y, Desk hr:ltd;
Note: luggage room, laundry, forex, a/c, central

Youth Hostel Pula, Zaljev Valsaline 4, Pula, Croatia; *www.hfhs.hr*, T:+385(0)52/391133, *pula@hfhs.hr*; $18bed, Kitchen:N, B'fast:Y, WiFi:Y, Pvt. room:N, Locker:N, Recep:ltd; Note: resto/bar, laundry, luggage ok, c.c. ok, town far near beach

Hostel Alma, Stankovićeva, Pula, Croatia; *hostel-alma.com/*, T:052540679, *dodi.giovana@gmail.com;* $22bed, Kitchen:Y, B'fast:N, WiFi:Y, Pvt. room:Y, Locker:Y, Recep:ltd; Note: pool, parking, laundry, luggage ok, forex, a/c, few staff, central

Apartments Golubic, De Franceschi 15, Pula, Croatia; *www.apartments-pula.com*, T:052505695, *golubic@apartments-pula.com;* $18bed, Kitchen:Y, B'fast:N, WiFi:N, Pvt room:Y, Locker:N, Recep:>10p;
Note: parking, laundry, a/c, walk to beach & center

SPLIT is Croatia's second city and the Dalmatian Coast's largest. As such it is the transportation hub for the region, with connections over land and sea. Its origins involve the construction of Roman Emperor Diocletian's retirement palace here, and after the fall of the Empire in 476, governance was handled variously by the Byzantines, Venetians, and Hungary, the Dalmatian coast an entity effectively separate from the Slavic Croatian hinterlands. The number of Croats continued increasing, though, so by the fall of Venice in 1797, they were a clear majority and upon the dissolution of Austria-Hungary after WWII, the area came under the rule of Croatia and Yugoslavia.

During WWII Split was fiercely anti-Fascist and pro-Tito, the emerging Communist strongman of Yugoslavia. Post-WWII Split fared better than most of Yugoslavia, with its prosperous shipyards. Croatia declared independence from Yugoslavia in 1991. Tourism is the main industry now. The historic center, part of the palace and a world heritage site, is the main attraction. Museums include the Meštrović Gallery, the Archaeological Museum, the Museum of Croatian Archaeological Monuments, the City Museum, the Art Gallery, and the Ethnographic Museum, housed in the Venetian Gothic town hall. By European standards the weather is sublime and the prices low.

www.visit-croatia.co.uk/split/

Tchaikovsky Hostel Split, Petra Ilica Cajkovskog 4, Split, Croatia; *tchaikovskyhostel.com/*, T:021317124, *info@tchaikovskyhostel.com*; $26bed, Kitchen:N, B'fast:N, WiFi:Y, Pvt.room:N, Locker:Y, Recep:>10p;
Note: luggage room, linen free, c.c. ok, a/c, travel desk, central, coffee/tea

CroParadise Blue Hostel, Culica Dvori 31, Split, Croatia; *www.croparadise.com/*, T:0914444194, *blue@croparadise.com;* $23bed, Kitchen:Y, B'fast:N, WiFi:Y, Pvt.room:Y, Locker:Y, Recep:>11p;
Note: laundry, bikes, TV, a/c, in old city, hard to find, multiple locations

Kamena Lodge, Don Petra Perosa 20, Mravince, Split, Croatia; *www.kamenalodge.com/*, T:021269910, *info@kamenalodge.com;* $26bed, Kitchen:Y, B'fast:$, WiFi:Y, Pvt. room:Y, Locker:Y, Recep:24/7;

Note: bar, pool, luggage room, laundry, travel desk, out of town, homey

Silver Central Hostel, Kralja Tomislava 1, Split, Croatia; *silvercentralhostel.com/*, T:0989955878, *silvercentralhostel@gmail.com;* $20bed, Kitchen:N, B'fast:N, WiFi:Y, Pvt.room:Y, Locker:Y, Recep:>11p;
Note: cash, luggage room, laundry, a/c, travel desk, pub crawl, central

Hostel Adria, Poljicka Cesta Jesenice, 58 Bajnice, Jesenice, Split; *www.hostel-adria.com*, T:+385911930722, *info@hostel-adria.com*; $26bed, Kitchen:Y, B'fast:Y, WiFi:Y, Pvt. room:Y, Locker:Y, Recep:ltd;
Note: coffee/tea, parking, TV, luggage ok, laundry, far from Split, on sea

Al's Place Hostel, Petra Kružića 10, Split, Croatia; *www.hostelsplit.com/*, T:0989182923, *info@hostelsplit.com;* $23bed, Kitchen:Y, B'fast:N, WiFi:N, Pvt.room:N, Locker:N, Recep:>9p;
Note: forex, laundry, luggage room, a/c, very small, pay Net no WiFi

Design Hostel Goli & Bosi, Morpurgova poljana 2, Split, Croatia; *http://gollybossy.com*, T:38521510999, *info@golibosi.com*; $27bed, Kitchen:N, B'fast:$, WiFi:Y, Pvt. room:Y, Locker:Y, Recep:24/7;
Note: resto/bar, luggage room, lift, wheelchair ok, a/c, c.c. ok, central

Silvergate Hostel, Hrvojeva 6, , Split, Croatia; *www.silvergatehostel.com/*, T:0989955878, *silvergatehostel@gmail.com;* $20bed, Kitchen:N, B'fast:N, WiFi:Y, Pvt. room:Y, Locker:Y, Recep:24/7;
Note: parking, luggage room, laundry, a/c, no bunks, good location

Split Hostel Booze & Snooze, Narodni trg 8, Split, Croatia; *www.splithostel.com/*, T:021342787, *info@splithostel.com*; $26bed, Kitchen:N, B'fast:N, WiFi:Y, Pvt. room:N, Locker:Y, Recep:ltd;
Note: 1N non-ref dep, advise arrival, a/c, travel desk, central, pub crawl

Hostel Ana, Hrvojeva 6, Split, Croatia;
www.hostel-ana.com/, T:021355032, *zahi_get@live.com;* $17bed, Kitchen:N, B'fast:N, WiFi:Y, Pvt. room:Y, Locker:N, Recep:24/7;
Note: laundry, a/c, good location, disorganized

Diocletian's Palace Hostel, Dioklecijanova 5, Split, Croatia;
www.diocletianpalace.com/, T: 098858141, *hostel@diocletianpalace.com;*
$20bed, Kitchen:N, B'fast:$, WiFi:Y, Pvt. room:Y, Locker:Y, Desk hr:24/7;
Note: age limit 45, resto/bar/café, lounge, TV, luggage ok, laundry, bikes

Hostel Split Backpackers, Kralja Zvonimira 17, Split, Croatia;
facebalkan.com/hostel-split, T:021782483, *splitbackpackers@gmail.com;*
$23bed, Kitchen:Y, B'fast:N, WiFi:Y, Pvt. room:Y, Locker:Y, Recep:ltd;
Note: near ferry/bus/train, luggage room, tour desk, a/c, c.c. ok

ZADAR was originally populated by pre-Indo-European speakers and became a city in Roman times. It thrived during the Byzantine era. Venice later fortified the city during the Renaissance era, but still the Ottomans attacked, and then the Austrians remodeled. Roman ruins survive to this day, including the forum. Other attractions are St. Donat's 9th C. circular church, St. Mary's Church and the Romanesque Church of St. Krševan, consecrated in 1175. There are also the 13th C. Cathedral of St. Stošija (Anastasia), and the Franciscan church and monastery. Zadar has an archaeological museum, the state archives, a theatre, and a small branch of the University of Zagreb. Tourism and maritime industries dominate the economy.

www.tzzadar.hr/en/

Hostel Elena, Ćirila Ivekovića 4, Zadar, Croatia;
www.hostel-elena-zadar.hr/, T:0915723439, *zlucic6@gmail.com;*
$23bed, Kitchen:Y, B'fast:N, WiFi:Y, Pvt room:N, Locker:Y, Recep:ltd;
Note: luggage room, a/c, in old city

Old Town Hostel, Mihe Klaića 5, Zadar, Croatia;
oldtownzadar.com/, T:0998093280, *oldtownzadar@gmail.com;* $21bed, Kitchen:Y, B'fast:N, WiFi:Y, Pvt room:Y, Locker:Y, Recep:>10p;

Note: cash, upper floors no lift, advise late arrival, laundry, TV, central

Drunken Monkey Hostel, Jure Kastriotića Skenderbega 21, Zadar; *www.drunkenmonkeyhostel.com/*, T:023314406; $31bed, Kitchen:Y, B'fast:N, WiFi:Y, Pvt room:Y, Locker:Y, Recep:ltd; Note: bar, pool, travel desk, parties, far from center, close to beach, cats

Youth Hostel Zadar, Obala kneza Trpimira 76, Zadar, Croatia; *www.hfhs.hr/en*, T:023331145, *info@hfhs.hr*; $19bed, Kitchen:N, B'fast:Y, WiFi:Y, Pvt.room:N, Locker:Y, Desk hr:>1a; Note: resto/bar, luggage ok, prkng, c.c. ok, not central, nr sea, no sign

ZAGREB is the capital and largest city of Croatia. It has been a city since at least the start of the last millennium, though a Roman city preceded it going back another thousand years at least. It was originally two cities—Gradec the fortress and Kaptol the church settlement—which gradually grew together. Gradec has the Gothic-style Church of St. Marcus, the Baroque Church of St. Catherine, the palaces of Zrinski and Oršić, and the Neoclassical Drasković Palace. Kaptol has the Gothic Cathedral of St. Stephen and the Baroque palace of the archbishops of Zagreb, with a chapel of St. Stephen. For culture there are the Academy of Sciences and Arts, the University of Zagreb, various museums and the Croatian National Theatre. It is well-connected to the rest of Europe, and while there is not the fun 'n sun of the coast, it is well worth a day or two or three.

www.zagreb.com/

Chillout Hostel Zagreb, Fra Andrije Kačića Miošića 3, Zagreb, Croatia; chillout-hostel-zagreb.com, T:014849605, *info@chillout-hostelzagreb.com*; $22bed, Kitchen:Y, B'fast:N, WiFi:Y, Pvt. room:N, Locker:Y, Recep:24/7; Note: café/bar, luggage room, forex. a/c, c.c. ok, new, central

Old Town Zagreb/Buzz BP, Đorđićeva 24, Zagreb, *buzzbackpackers.com*, **T:**014816748, *oldtownzagreb@buzzbackpackers.com;* $23bed,

Kitchen:Y, B'fast:N, WiFi:Y, Pvt. room:Y, Locker:Y, Recep:>11p;
Note: coffee/tea, laundry, luggage room, forex, travel desk, no-party

Funk Lounge, Ivana Rendića 28, Zagreb, Croatia;
www.funklounge.hr/, T:015552707, *recepcija@funklounge.hr*; $24bed,
Kitchen:Y, B'fast:N, WiFi:Y, Pvt. room:Y, Locker:Y, Recep:24/7;
Note: luggage room, a/c, cash, supermarket close, central

Funk Hostel & Club, Poljička 13, Zagreb, Croatia;
www.funkhostel.hr/, T:016314530, *recepcija@gunkhostel.hr*; $24bed,
Kitchen:Y, B'fast:Y, WiFi:Y, Pvt. room:N, Locker:Y, Recep:24/7;
Note: bar, prkng, laundry, central, bikes, travel desk, a/c, c.c. ok, smokin'

Hostel Nocturno, Skalinska 2a, Zagreb, Croatia; *www.nokturno.hr/*;
$25bed, Kitchen:Y, B'fast:N, WiFi:Y, Pvt. room:Y, Locker:Y,
Recep:24/7;
Note: coffee & tea, bike rent, laundry, good location, hot in summer

Buzz Hostel, Babukićeva 1b, Zagreb, Croatia; *buzzbackpackers.com/*,
T:012320267, *reception@buzzbackpackers.com*; $21bed,
Kitchen:N, B'fast:N, WiFi:Y, Pvt room:Y, Locker:Y, Recep:ltd;
Note: luggage room, forex, travel desk, a/c, coffee & tea, near center

Fulir Hostel, Pavla Radića 3, Zagreb, Croatia;
www.fulir-hostel.com/, T:014830882, *fulir@fulir-hostel.com*; $17bed,
Kitchen:Y, B'fast:N, WiFi:Y, Pvt room:Y, Locker:Y, Recep:>10p;
Note: laundry, luggage room, central

Ravnice Y.H., Ravnice 1 38, Zagreb, *www.ravnice-youth-hostel.hr*,
T:012332325, *ravnice-youth-hostel@zg.t-com.hr*; $20bed,
Kitchen:Y, B'fast:Y, WiFi:Y, Pvt. room:Y, Locker:Y, Recep:>10p;
Note: luggage room, laundry, parking, TV, activities, far from center

Hostel Mali Mrak Zagreb, Dubicka 8, Zagreb, Croatia;
www.hostel-zagreb.com/, T:+38516389109; $19bed,
Kitchen:N, B'fast:N, WiFi:Y, Pvt. room:Y, Locker:Y, Recep:24/7;

Note: luggage room, laundry, forex, a/c, c.c. OK, not central

Youth Hostel Zagreb, Petrinjska Street no. 77, Zagreb, Croatia; *www.hfhs.hr*, T:+385(0)14841261, *zagreb@hfhs.hr*; $22bed, Kitchen:N, B'fast:N, WiFi:Y, Pvt. room:N, Locker:Y, Recep:24/7; Note: discount for members, not far

Hostel Lika, Pašmanska 17, Zagreb, Croatia; *www.hostel-lika.com/*, T:098561041, *hostel-lika@yahoo.com*; $18bed, Kitchen:N, B'fast:$, WiFi:Y, Pvt. room:Y, Locker:Y, Recep:>10p; Note: laundry, parking, a/c, bar

8) Cyprus

Cyprus is an island in the Mediterranean Sea that lies less than a hundred miles from the shores of Turkey, Syria, and Lebanon. Its culture, though, is predominantly Greek, and has been for millennia. Then the Ottoman Turks invaded in 1570. Since then it has been culturally divided, though it became independent after years of British protection in 1960. In 1974 the country became politically divided, too, which is where it stands today, divided between a Europeanized southern Greek half and a northern Turkish half. Turkish and Greek are languages; Cyprus pound (CYP) is currency; calling code is +357.

www.visitcyprus.com

KYRENIA is capital of the northern Turkish half of the island. There is a 12th C. castle fortress with the remains of a ship dating to 300 BC. Nearby in the Kyrenia Mountains are the 13th C. Abbey of Bellapais and the fortress of St. Hilarion. Besides Turkish Cypriots, British citizens are in abundance.

discoverkyrenia.net/

Cyprus Dorms, Above Set Balik Restaurant, 6 Bozaklar Sok;
cyprusdorms.com/, T:05338872007; $13bed, Kitchen:Y,
B'fast:$, WiFi:Y, Pvt. room:Y, Locker:Y, Desk hr:ltd;
Note: laundry, forex, a/c, good location, terrace views, UN ok'd

9) Czech Republic

The Czech Republic is the other Eastern European nation—besides Poland and Hungary—most intertwined with the West historically, and long a constituent part of the Habsburg Empire and its successor Austria-Hungary. Before that, as Bohemia, it was part of the Great Moravian Empire, then the Holy Roman Empire. Upon integration into the Habsburg monarchy it was subjected to forced "Germanization" and eventual industrialization. After WWI it became one-half of Czechoslovakia and after WWII became a Communist-ruled part of the Warsaw Pact. It always chafed at the bit, though, and the Prague Spring of 1968 fired the first (okay, second after Hungary) shot across the bow of the Soviet hulk to signal that all was not right in the Empire. That was crushed brutally but twenty years later it was more like velvet crush in the Velvet Revolution of 1989 that brought down the Communists and eventually separated the Czechs and Slovaks back into their constituent republics.

Today the Czech Republic is a fully developed country, democratic and healthy and tourist central. Interestingly, for such a small country, rivers from the Czech Republic drain into three different seas. The country itself is entirely landlocked, except for a lot on the Hamburg docks awarded to it by the Treaty of Versailles. I bet the Reeperbahn is close by. Did I mention that this is ancient Bohemia? Yes, the beer is good. Yes, you can get one for breakfast. No, you won't be alone. There are also castles and spas. Czech music and literature are among the best. Czech is the language; *koruna* (CZK) is currency, and the calling code is +420.

www.czechtourism.com/

BRNO is the Czech Republic's second city and an important university town. It is in the eastern Moravian part of the country, so not quite so Bohemian. Its history extends back to a Middle Age fortified settlement in an area where Celtic and Germanic tribes had lived previously. It soon would become one of the major cities of Moravia. Like the rest of central Europe, the main historical drama was the struggle between Germans, Slavs, and Jews. WWII settled all that, with the loss of Brno's 12,000 Jews and the expulsion of Germans. Today it is an important exhibition and trade center. It has historical sites, festivals, and nature to enjoy, first among them Spilberk Castle, the Cathedral of Saints Peter and Paul, and the Moravian Karst formations. Since the fall of Communism, it has undergone a cultural rebirth, including the revival of old traditions. Some of the finest surviving buildings include the churches of St. Thomas and St. James, the Augustinian monastery, and Tugendhat House, a World Heritage Site.

www.ticbrno.cz

Hostel Mitte, Panská 11, Brno, Czech Republic;
www.hostelmitte.com, T:+420734622340, *info@hostelmitte.com*; $26bed,
Kitchen:Y, B'fast:Y, WiFi:Y, Pvt. room:Y, Locker:Y, Recep:ltd;
Note: bar, luggage room, c.c. ok, central, close to train

Hostel Fleda, Štefánikova 24, Brno, Czech Republic;
www.hostelfleda.com, T:+420533433638, *info@hostelfleda.com;* $16bed,
Kitchen:Y, B'fast:$, WiFi:Y, Pvt. room:Y, Locker:Y, Recep:ltd;
Note: laundry, bar/club, c.c. ok, old house, noise from downstairs bar

CESKE BUDEJOVICE is also known as Budweis, with all that name represents, mostly beer. The American and Czech brands are not the same. There is also historic architecture if you need something to look at while getting happy, including an arcaded town square and the Baroque Samson's Fountain. There's a Museum of South Bohemia.

www.czechtourism.com/

Cuba Bar & Hostel, Nová 2024/18, 370 10 České Budějovice 3, Czech;
www.cuba-bar.cz/, T:777723803, *info@cuba-bar.cz;* $15bed,
Kitchen:Y, B'fast:N, WiFi:Y, Pvt. room:Y, Locker:Y, Recep:5p>;
Note: check-in at bar, laundry, parking

CESKY KRUMLOV is a medieval town complete with a castle of the same name that is second in size only to Hradcany (Prague Castle) complex in Prague, unusual for such a small town. The Castle Theatre is especially nice. It has historically been a part of the German-speaking Sudetenland, and therefore subject to frequent political drama. There are cultural festivals. On summer solstice the entire town dresses in medieval costume.

www.ckrumlov.info

Hostel Krumlov House, Rooseveltova 68, Cesky Krumlov, Czech Rep; *www.krumlovhostel.com/*, T:+420380711935, *info@krumlovhostel.com*; $18bed, Kitchen:Y, B'fast:N, WiFi:Y, Pvt. room:Y, Locker:Y, Recep:ltd; Note: luggage room, laundry, parking

Hostel 99, Věžní 99, Český Krumlov, Czech Republic; *www.hostel99.cz,/*, T:380712812, *hostel99@hostel99.cz*; $18bed, Kitchen:Y, B'fast:N, WiFi:Y, Pvt. room:N, Locker:Y, Recep:9a>9p; Note: resto/bar, parking, laundry, coffee & tea

Hostel Merlin, Kájovská 59, Český Krumlov, Czech Republic; *www.hostelmerlin.com/en*, T:606256145, *info@hostelmerlin.com*; $13bed, Kitchen:Y, B'fast:N, WiFi:Y, Pvt room:Y, Locker:N, Recep:11a>8p; Note: parking, coffee & tea

Travellers Hostel Soukenicka, Soukenická 43, Český Krumlov; *www.travellers.cz*, T:380711345, *krumlov@travellers.cz*; $16bed, Kitchen:Y, B'fast:$, WiFi:Y, Pvt. room:Y, Locker:Y, Recep:ltd; Note: resto/bar, laundry, c.c. ok

Hostel Havana, U Svateho Ducha 135, Cesky Krumlov, C.R.; *havanahostels.cz/*, T:+420777723244, *info@havanahostels.cz;* $13bed, Kitchen:Y, B'fast:N, WiFi:Y, Pvt. room:Y, Locker:Y, Recep:ltd; Note: travel desk, parking, quiet, garden

OLOMOUC is the historic capital of Moravia and sixth largest city in the Czech Republic today. Aside from the usual jockeying for position between locals, Germans, and Jews, Olomouc has also played the fall guy for Swedes during their empire and the Prussians during theirs. Being the capital is dangerous. There are several historical ecclesiastical monuments and a torture rack. Historic buildings include the 14th C. Gothic St. Wenceslas' Cathedral, and the town hall, with an astronomical clock. Notable fountains are Triton and Caesar's. Holy Trinity Column, a UNESCO World Heritage site, is an example of the Olomouc Baroque style.

tourism.olomouc.eu

Poets Corner Hostel, Sokolská 1, Olomouc, Czech Republic; *www.hostelolomouc.com*; T:777570730; $17bed, Kitchen:Y, B'fast:N, WiFi:Y, Pvt. room:Y, Locker:Y, Recep:ltd; Note: luggage room, laundry, tour desk, central

PILSEN is the Czech Republic's fourth city and is located in the western Bohemian part of the country, only 55mi/90 km west of Prague. It is a trade and industrial center and once had large populations of Germans and Jews. There are important cathedrals and synagogues and lots of beer, the ones that made it famous. Landmarks are St. Bartholomew's church, the Franciscan Church of the Virgin Mary, and the Renaissance town hall.

www.pilsen.eu

Euro Hostel Pilsen, Na Roudne 13, Pilsen, Czech Republic; *www.eurohostel.cz*, T:+420377259926, *info@eurohostel.cz*; $21bed, Kitchen:N, B'fast:$, WiFi:Y, Pvt. room:Y, Locker:Y, Desk hr:24/7; Note: restaurant, prkng, laundry, luggage room, travel desk

Hostel River, Černická 625/12, Plzeň, Czech Republic; *www.hostelriver.com*, T:774082790, *hostelriver@seznam.cz*; $20bed, Kitchen:Y, B'fast:N, WiFi:Y, Pvt. room:Y, Locker:N, Recep:ltd; Note: parking, luggage room, central, coffee & tea, cash only, TV

PRAGUE sits on a prime piece of Vitava River real estate that was occupied by Celtic tribes, then Germanic, before Slavic ones came in during the great migrations that followed the post-Roman era in Europe. Merchants would settle here just to trade, and by the ninth century were in place the beginnings of Prague Castle, then bridges, then cathedrals. Germans had their neighborhoods, as did Jews, but this was not without tensions, especially when the Industrial Revolution increased wealth and defined social classes. When Hitler entered Czechoslovakia in 1939 (and the West did nothing), Prague's fate was sealed, for a while at least. At war's end, Prague was the capital of a Soviet-occupied tank-filled Czechoslovakia that not even "Prague Spring" could change. Today it is the main tourist destination in the Czech Republic, it being one of the first cities behind the former "Iron Curtain" that Western tourists, mostly young, flocked to and started *ad hoc* colonies for the purposes of low-budget partying.

The city is friendly and the architecture is stunning. The entire historic center is a UNESCO world heritage site, and there are some 2000 recognized monuments. Some of the highlights are Charles Bridge, the castle of Hradčany (Prague Castle), Old Town, Wenceslas Square, the Jewish Quarter, the Church of St. George, St. Vitus' Cathedral, the Týn Church on Staroměstské ("Old Town") Square, Powder Tower, Bethlehem Chapel, St. Agnes Convent, the Old-New Synagogue, the Old Jewish Cemetery, Valdštejn and Clam-Gallas palaces, St. Nicholas Church, the Antonín Dvořák Museum, the Golz-Kinský Palace, the Bedřich Smetana Museum, the Belvedere Palace, the National Museum, the National Theatre... and of course Lennon Wall, testament to Prague's long flirtation with Lennonism even in the darkest days of Stalinism. By modern standards Prague's hostels are now of only decent quality, the best and brightest now elsewhere.

www.praha.eu/

Art Hole Hostel, Soukenická 1756/34, Prague 1-Nové Město; *www.artholehostel.com/*, T:222314028, *info@artholehostel.com*; $23bed, Kitchen:Y, B'fast:Y, WiFi:Y, Pvt. room:N, Locker:Y, Recep:24/7; Note: close to old town, age restrictions

Hostel One Prague, Cimburkova 916/8, Prague 3-Žižkov; *www.hosteloneprague.com/*, T:222221423, *hostelprague@gmail.com*; $15bed, Kitchen:Y, B'fast:N, WiFi:Y, Pvt.room:Y, Locker:Y, Recep:>12m; Note: lift, café, bike rent, free tour/travel desk, laundry, luggage room, TV

Czech Inn, Francouzská 76, Praha 10, Prague, Czech Republic; *www.czech-inn.com/*, T:+420267267612, *info@czech-inn.com*; $15bed, Kitchen:N, B'fast:$, WiFi:Y, Pvt. room:Y, Locker:Y, Recep:24/7; Note: c.c. +4%, bar/café, lift, ATM, luggage room, laundry, not central

Miss Sophie's, Melounova 3, Prague, Czech Republic; *www.miss-sophies.com/*, T:296303530, *info@miss-sophies.com*; $25bed, Kitchen:Y, B'fast:$, WiFi:Y, Pvt. room:Y, Locker:Y, Recep:24/7; Note: c.c. +4%, luggage room, safe deposit, central

Hostel Miles, Vodičkova 38, Praha, Czech Republic; *hostelmiles.com/*, T:+420773800732, *robert@hostelmiles.com*; $20bed, Kitchen:Y, B'fast:N, WiFi:Y, Pvt. room:Y, Locker:Y, Recep:24/7; Note: lift, forex, free tour, a/c, c.c. ok, luggage room, laundry, central

Hostel Orange, Vaclavske namesti 20, Prague, Czech Republic; *www.hostelorange.com/*, T:+420223018557, *Hostelorange20@gmail.com*; $18bed, Kitchen:Y, B'fast:$, WiFi:Y, Pvt. room:Y, Locker:Y, Recep:>11p;
Note: resto/bar/club, prkng, free tour/info, forex c.c. ok, central, no sign

Hostel Lipa, Tachovské náměstí 288/6, Prague 3-Žižkov, Czech Rep; *www.hostellipa.com/*, T:602211182, *info@hostellipa.com*; $18bed, Kitchen:Y, B'fast:N, WiFi:Y, Pvt. room:Y, Locker:Y, Recep:ltd; Note: restaurant, wheelchair ok, prkng, Jacuzzi, not central, microbrew

Hostel Downtown, Národní 19, Praha 2, Prague, Czech Republic; *www.hostel-downtown.cz*, T:(+420)224240570, *downtown@jsc.cz;* $25bed, Kitchen:Y, B'fast:$, WiFi:Y, Pvt. room:Y, Locker:Y, Recep:24/7;
Note: free tour/info, luggage room, laundry, c.c. ok, non-party, central

Little Town, Malostranské náměstí 260/11, Prague 1, Czech Rep; *www.littletownhotel.cz/en/*, T:242406965, *info@littletownhotel.cz*; $24bed, Kitchen:Y, B'fast:$, WiFi:Y, Pvt. room:Y, Locker: Y, Recep:24/7; Note: resto/bar/club, free tour, travel desk, close to castle, laundry, c.c. ok

Hostel Mango, Míšeňská 68/8, Prague 1-Malá Strana, Czech Rep; *www.hostelmango.com/en/*, T:776238563, *hostelmango@gmail.com*; $19bed, Kitchen:Y, B'fast:$, WiFi:Y, Pvt. room:Y, Locker:Y, Recep:ltd; Note: café/resto/bar/club, free tour, travel desk, luggage room, central

Sir Toby's Hostel, Dělnická 1155/24, Praha 7-Holešovice, Czech Rep; *www.sirtobys.com/*, T:246032611; $15bed, Kitchen:Y, B'fast:$, WiFi:Y, Pvt. room:Y, Locker:N, Desk hr:24/7; Note: bar, parking, free tour, luggage room, laundry, c.c. ok, un-central

St. Christopher's at Mosaic House, Odboru 4, Prague, Czech Republic; *www.mosaichouse.com/*, T:+420246008324, *info@mosaichouse.com*; $23bed, Kitchen:N, B'fast:N, WiFi:Y, Pvt. room:Y, Locker:Y, Recep:24/7; Note: wheelchair ok, resto/bar, travel desk, luggage ok, forex, c.c. ok

Hostel Rosemary, Růžová 971/5, Prague 1-Nové Město, Czech Republic; *www.praguecityhostel.cz/en/*, T:222211124, *info@praguecityhostel.cz*; $17bed, Kitchen:Y, B'fast:N, WiFi:Y, Pvt. room:Y, Locker:N, Recep:>7p;Note: lift, laundry, luggage room, free tour, travel desk, c.c. ok, central

Little Quarter Hostel, Nerudova 246/21, Prague 1-Malá Strana, Czech R; *www.littlequarter.com/*, T:257212029, *LQ@avehotels.cz*; $26bed, Kitchen:Y, B'fast:$, WiFi:Y, Pvt. room:Y, Locker:Y, Desk hr:24/7; Note: no bunks, luggage ok, travel desk, forex, c.c. ok, tourist district

Plus Prague Hostel, Přívozní 1562/1, Praha-Holešovice, Czech Rep; *www.plushostels.com/plusprague*, T:220510046; $21bed, Kitchen:N, B'fast:$, WiFi:Y, Pvt. room:Y, Locker:Y, Recep:24/7;
Note: resto/bar/club, prkng, luggage ok, forex, c.c. ok, pool, sauna

Prague Sqare Hostel, Melantrichova 471/10, Prague 1-Old Town. C.R.; *praguesquarehostel.com/*, T:224240859, *info@praguesquarehostel.com*; $24bed, Kitchen:Y, B'fast:Y, WiFi:Y, Pvt. room:Y, Locker:Y, Recep:24/7;
Note: resto/bar/club, luggage room, travel desk, central

Hostel Marabou, Koněvova 738/55, Žižkov, Prague, Czech Rep; *www.hostelmarabou.com/*, T:222581182, *info@hostelmarabou.com*; $16bed, Kitchen:Y, B'fast:Y, WiFi:Y, Pvt. room:Y, Locker:Y, Recep:24/7;
Note: bar, free tour, forex, c.c. ok, 2.5mi/4km from old town, smoking

Advantage Hostel, Sokolská 11, Prague, Czech Republic; *www.advantagehostel.cz*, T:739343864, *advantage@jsc.cz*; $25bed, Kitchen:Y, B'fast:Y, WiFi:Y, Pvt. room:Y, Locker:Y, Recep:24/7;
Note: resto/bar, free tour/info, bikes, luggage ok, laundry, c.c. ok, TV

Royal Road Residence, Karlova 20, Prague, Czech Republic; *www.prагueroyalroad.com/*, T:602167441, *info@pragueallsuites.com*; $25bed, Kitchen:Y, B'fast:$, WiFi:Y, Pvt.room:Y, Locker:Y, Recep:>10p;
Note: bar, parking, forex, overbooks go elsewhere, laundry, a/c, c.c. ok

Riverbank Hostel, Masarykovo nábřeží 2016/6, Praha 4 NewTown; *riverbank.cz/*, T:724879687, *info.riverbank@yahoo.com*; $15bed, Kitchen:Y, B'fast:N, WiFi:Y, Pvt. room:Y, Locker:Y, Recep:ltd;
Note: luggage room, check-in elsewhere, view of river, central

Travellers Hostel Dlouha, Dlouhá 33, Prague 1, Czech Republic; *www.travellers.cz*, T:224826663, *hostel@travellers.cz*; $14bed, Kitchen:Y, B'fast:Y, WiFi:Y, Pvt, room:Y, Locker:Y, Recep:24/7;
Note: wheelchair ok, bar, luggage room, laundry, c.c. ok, central

Hostel Clown & Bard, Bořivojova 102, Praha 3, Czech Republic; *www.clownandbard.com*, T:222716453, *horek@clownandbard.com*; $12bed, Kitchen:Y, B'fast:$, WiFi:Y, Pvt. room:Y, Locker:Y, Recep:24/7;
Note: cash, smoking in bar, free tour/info, luggage room, forex, uncentral

Hostel Marrakesh, Biskupská 1139/4, Prague 1-Nové Město, C R; *hostelmarrakesh.com/*, T:734373425, *info@hostelmarrakesh.com*; $14bed, Kitchen:Y, B'fast:Y, WiFi:Y, Pvt. room:N, Locker:N, Recep:ltd;
Note: free tour/info, forex, ATM, luggage room, a/c, c.c. ok, staff scarce

Hostel Aplus Hotel, Na Florenci 1413/33, Praha 1, Czech Republic; *www.aplus-hostel.cz*, T:222314272, *info@aplus-hostel.cz*; $15bed, Kitchen:Y, B'fast:Y, WiFi:Y, Pvt. room:N, Locker:Y, Recep:24/7;
Note: resto/bar/club, tour desk, luggage ok, laundry, cc ok, 10-min walk

Emma Hostel, Na Zderaze 267/10, Prague-New Town, Czech Rep; *hostel-emma.com/*, T:222521269, *emmahostel@yahoo.com*; $11bed, Kitchen:Y, B'fast:N, WiFi:Y, Pvt. room:Y, Locker:N, Recep:24/7;
Note: free tour, travel desk, parking, luggage room, pets ok, central

Pension Tara, Havelska 15, Praha 1, Prague, Czech Republic; *www.pensiontara.net/en/*, T:+420224228083, *info@pensiontara.net*; $26bed, Kitchen:N, B'fast:$, WiFi:Y, Pvt. room:Y, Locker:Y, Recep:ltd;
Note: restaurant, free tour/info, historical, c.c. ok, stairs no lift, central

Euro Guesthouse, Krakovska 3, Praha 1, Prague, Czech Republic; *www.euroguesthouse.eu*, T:+420608414422; $24bed, Kitchen:Y, B'fast:N, WiFi:Y, Pvt. room:Y, Locker:N, Recep:9a>9p;
Note: arpt pickup, resto/bar, free tour, overbooks to Hostel 123, center

Sokolska Youth Hostel, 52 Sokolska str., Prague, Czech Republic; *www.hostel52.com/*, T:+420252546181, *hostel52@gmail.com*; $14bed, Kitchen:Y, B'fast:$, WiFi:Y, Pvt. room:Y, Locker:N, Recep:24/7;
Note: restaurant, parking, free tour/info, luggage room, c.c. ok, central
Hostel City Center, Ječná 509/12, Prague 4-Nové Město, Czech Rep; *www.hostel-citycenter.cz/*, T:420266315266, *info@hostel-citycenter.cz*;

$16bed, Kitchen:N, B'fast:$, WiFi:Y, Pvt. room:Y, Locker:N, Recep:24/7;
Note: tour desk, luggage room, parking, c.c. ok, central

Penzion Sprint, Cukrovarnicka 64, Prague, Czech Republic; *www.penzionsprint.cz*, T:+420233344871, *penzionsprint@iol.cz*; $11bed, Kitchen:Y, B'fast:$, WiFi:Y, Pvt. room:Y, Locker:N, Recep:24/7;
Note: resto-bar, tour desk, laundry, luggage ok, parking, c.c, uncentral

TREBIC is a small Moravian city, centrally located in the Czech Republic. It is famous for its Jewish Quarter and St. Procopius Basilica, both UNESCO world heritage sites.

www.visittrebic.eu

Travellers Hostel, Žerotínovo námestí 19, Trebic, Czech Republic; *www.travellers.cz*, T:(420)568422594, *trebic@www.travellers.cz*; $13bed, Kitchen:Y, B'fast:Y, WiFi:Y, Pvt. room:Y, Locker:Y, Recep:ltd;
Note: UNESCO Jewish quarter, resto/bar, luggage room, laundry, c.c. ok

ZNOJMO is on the border with Austria, less than two hours from Vienna, and overlooks the Dyje River. There is a castle, historic churches, and catacombs. The entire old town is an ancient monument, with many medieval buildings.

www.znojmocity.cz

Travellers Hostel, Stare Mesto 22, Znojmo, Czech Republic; *www.travellers.cz*, T:(+420)515221489, *znojmo@travellers.cz*; $16bed, Kitchen:Y, B'fast:Y, WiFi:Y, Pvt. room:Y, Locker:Y, Recep:ltd;
Note: central

10) Estonia

Estonia shares much of the same history as its Baltic buddies Latvia and Lithuania, but that is mostly circumstantial, a sharing of the same events of the last millennium—Vikings, Hansesatic League, Germans and Russians, Nazism and Communism. Its genetic roots lie with Finland across the water—language and presumably DNA, united at a time in the past in a place to the east, a time and place that must have included the Magyars of Hungary in its orbit, if linguistic evidence is to believed. That all predates the historic record, though, so must go back at least a few thousand years. Still I think it's reasonable to assume that the Finns and Estonians were here first, before the Indo-European Scandinavians. Sami (Lapp) is another related language by the way. The Roman historian Tacitus mentions the *Aesti* as amber traders. Later evidence indicates a Viking presence here, though it's not clear in what capacity, as native Estonian "Osselian pirates" would seem to be their competition.

Later Teutons, Swedes, and Russians all pretty much had their way here as they did elsewhere in the Baltics. Then the citizens of all three Baltic countries united in a human chain to protest Soviet occupation in 1989. Today Estonia is a post-USSR success story, a "Baltic Tiger," ready to rock and ready to work. It has carefully been promoting itself as "Nordic," not "Baltic" (i.e.winners not losers). The economy is market-oriented. Politics are liberal and democratic. Protestant work ethic is strong, though hardly anyone is religious. Skype™ was developed here. Music and song festivals are an important tradition. Euro (EUR) is currency; Estonian is the language, phone code +372.

www.visitestonia.com/en/

TALLINN, formerly known as Reval, is the principal city of Estonia in every way. It was a Hanseatic city back in the day, and something like a time capsule today. If nothing else, communism can be depended on to stop the clock. It is also party central for mobile hip Westerners who like to descend on a budget-friendly member of their European hinterlands which has just been selected for further in-depth maneuvers of the social kind… all of which is to say that the women are friendly. The city is cute as a bug, too, and a UNESCO world heritage site. Landmarks include the 13th C. Toom Church, the Gothic Oleviste and Niguliste churches, the Great Guildhall of 1410, the 14th C. Rathus, and much of the old castle. It is well-connected by ferry to Finland, Russia, and Germany, by bus to the south, and budget airlines to all over. Hostels are good, but please, "don't sleep drunk in the kitchen." And don't sleep on the router, either.

www.tourism.tallinn.ee/eng

Red Emperor Hostel, Aia 10, Tallinn, Estonia;
redemperorhostel.com/, T:58091576, *craig@redemperorhostel.com*;
$21bed, Kitchen:Y, B'fast:$, WiFi:Y, Pvt. room:Y, Locker:N,
Recep:24/7;
Note: bar, parking, free tour, travel desk, laundry, luggage room, c.c. ok

Tallinn Backpackers, Olevimägi 11, Tallinn, Estonia;
www.tallinnbackpackers.com, T:6166754, *info@tallinnbackpackers.com*;
$23bed, Kitchen:Y, B'fast:N, WiFi:Y, Pvt. room:N, Locker:Y,
Recep:24/7;
Note: bar, free tour, travel desk, laundry, luggage ok, c.c. ok, parties

The Monk's Bunk, Tatari 1, Tallinn, Estonia;
www.themonksbunk.com, T:6561120, *info@themonksbunk.com*; $16bed,
Kitchen:Y, B'fast:N, WiFi:Y, Pvt. room:Y, Locker:Y, Recep:24/7;
Note: bar, free tour/info, c.c. ok, luggage ok, laundry, near center, party

Old House Hostel, Uus 26, Tallinn, Estonia;
www.oldhouse.ee, T:+3726411281, *info@oldhouse.ee*; $13bed,
Kitchen:Y, B'fast:$, WiFi:Y, Pvt. room:Y, Locker:N, Desk hr:24/7;
Note: parking, safe deposit, no bunks, in old town

Gidic Backpackers, 31 Tartu mnt, Tallinn, Estonia;
www.gidic.ee/, T:+3736466016, *bookings@gidic.ee*; $17bed,
Kitchen:Y, B'fast:$, WiFi:Y, Pvt. room:Y, Locker:Y, Desk hr:24/7;
Note: bike rent, free tour, fax, luggage room, laundry, c.c. ok, parking

ALUR Hostel Tallinn Old Town, Lai 20, Kesklinn, Harju County;
hostel.alur.ee, T:6466210, *hostel.alur@gmail.com*; $17bed,
Kitchen:Y, B'fast:$, WiFi:Y, Pvt. room:Y, Locker:N, Recep 24/7;
Note: free tour, travel desk, luggage room, c.c. ok, old town

Flying Kiwi Backackers, Nunne 1, Tallinn, Estonia;
www.flyingkiwitallinn.com/, T:58213292, *info@flyingkiwitallinn.com*;
$19bed, Kitchen:Y, B'fast:N, WiFi:Y, Pvt. room:Y, Locker:N, Recep:ltd;
Note: sauna, travel desk, old town

Teko Hostel, Lastekodu 13, Tallinn, Estonia;
www.hihostels.com/, T:+3726811352, *hostel@teeninduskool.ee*, $17bed,
Kitchen:Y, B'fast:Y, WiFi:Y, Pvt. room:Y, Locker:N, Recep:24/7;
Note: parking, store, TV, meals, luggage room, close to bus not center

16EUR Hostel, Roseni 9, Tallinn, Estonia;
www.16eur.ee, T:+3725013046, *info@16eur.ee*; $13bed,
Kitchen:Y, B'fast:$, WiFi:Y, Pvt. room:Y, Locker:Y, Recep:24/7;
Note: pool, bar, forex, luggage room, tour desk, c.c. ok

The Dancing Eesti, Väike-Karja 1, Tallinn, Estonia;
www.thedancingeesti.ee, T:53654382, *deniz@homemail.com*; $13bed,
Kitchen:Y, B'fast:N, WiFi:Y, Pvt. room:N, Locker:Y, Recep:24/7;
Note: left luggage, laundry, free tour/info, a/c, pub crawls, central

Kaupmehe Guest House, Kaupmehe 8, Tallinn, Estonia;
www.kaupmehe.com/, T:+37255535722, *s.belosapko@gmail.com*;
$11bed, Kitchen:Y, B'fast:N, WiFi:Y, Pvt. room:N, Locker:N, Recep:ltd;
Note: call to check in, laundry, hard to find, staff scarce, close to center

TARTU is Estonia's second city and a university town, the intellectual and cultural counterpoint to Tallinn's political and financial orientation.

First documented in the chronicles of Kievan Rus, it also went through the same phases in the Hanseatic League and regional rivalries as Tallinn. Architecture shows influence from Germans and Russians.

www.tartu.ee/

Terviseks, Raekoja Plats 10, Tartu, Estonia;
www.terviseksbbb.com, T:+3725655382, *terviseksbbb@gmail.com*;
$20bed, Kitchen:Y, B'fast:Y, WiFi:Y, Pvt. room:Y, Locker:Y, Recep:ltd;
Note: advise arrival time, central, laundry, free printing

Looming Hostel, Kastani 38, Tartu, Estonia;
loominghostel.ee/, T:(+372)56994398, *info@loominghostel.ee*; $20bed;
Kitchen:Y, B'fast:$, WiFi:Y, Pvt. room:N, Locker:Y, Recep:ltd;
Note: bike rent, luggage room, tour desk, parking, pets ok, eco-artsy

HIIE MAJA, *Hiie* 10, *Tartu*, Estonia;
www.bed.ee, T:+3727421236, *info@bed.ee*; $20bed,
Kitchen:Y, B'fast:$, WiFi:Y, Pvt. room:Y, Locker:N, Recep:ltd;
Note: parking, camping ok, half hour walk to center

11) Georgia

Georgia is one of the three modern nations of the Caucasus, and none fits the image better, as one hodge-podge of ancient cultures with murky histories and many languages. Georgia itself corresponds to the ancient countries of Iberia and Colchis, and today includes the breakaway provinces of Abkhazia and South Ossetia. Georgians themselves are likely directly descended from the autochtonous aboriginals of the regions together with whatever admixtures that came into creative conjunction when the nights were long and the weather was cold. That is likely not the case with the Altaic Azeris of Azerbaijan or the Indo-European Armenians. Ever wonder what happened to the ancient Scyths, Avars and Sarmatians? They're all here in the neighborhood. Interestingly some linguists have posited a connection between ancient Iberian Georgia and modern Iberian Basque. Others of us posit a connection between all of them. It adopted Christianity in the fourth century. Casinos are now ubiquitous. The Georgian language is Kartvelian, though languages like Mongol and Greek are also spoken in the region. *Lari* (GEL) is the currency; calling code is +995.

www.caucasustravel.com

TBILISI is Georgia's capital and largest city, and home to over a hundred ethnicities. In the same neighborhood, you can see churches, synagogues, and mosques. If that sounds like a typical immigrant magnet, well, it's always been that way here. Tbilisi was named for the numerous hot springs here, so maybe that's why so many different people came and left some baggage behind—Persia, Byzantines, Arabs, and Turks. The 12th century was Georgia's "golden age," until the Mongols came in 1236 and stayed for a century. Then the plague hit in 1366, as it did almost everywhere else in Europe (though apparently least in the Slavic countries with *banya*).

After that it was the bone of contention between Persians, Turks, and Russians until the modern era. Pick your master; Tbilisi was a predominately Armenian city at the time by the way.

After the Russian Revolution of 1917, Tbilisi briefly became capital of a united Transcaucasus of the three republics, then came independence, and then Russia invaded and made it a Soviet Socialist Republic a few short years later. You probably know the rest. Ex-Soviet foreign minister Eduard Shevardnadze became president in 1993 and presided over a period filled with crime, corruption, and chaos. After a rigged election, the people finally got their "Rose Revolution" in 2003. Things are better now. It is a pleasant modern city, but good luck walking around looking for a cheap hotel. That's why you need this book. Historic sights include the Nankala Fortress, Anchiskati Church, Sioni Cathedral, and Church of Mekheti. This is the connection point between Azerbaijan and Armenia, unless you're going through Iran. Direct border crossings between them are closed because of Nagorno-Karabakh.

world66.com/europe/georgia/tbilisi

Tbilisi Hostel, Georgia, Tbilisi, Avlabari, Makhati shesakhvevi 22; *tbilisihostel.com*, T:+995598551565, *tbilisi.hostel@gmail.com*; $11bed, Kitchen:Y, B'fast:N, WiFi:Y, Pvt. room:Y, Locker:Y, Recep:24/7; Note: bar, forex, laundry, luggage room, a/c, parking, partying

Tbilisi Friends Hostel, Old Tbilisi, Betlemi St. #28-30, Tbilisi; *www.friendshostel.ge/*, T:(8)555507705, *info@friendshostel.ge*; $12bed, Kitchen:Y, B'fast:$, WiFi:Y, Pvt. room:Y, Locker:Y, Recep:24/7; Note: bar, parking, laundry, luggage room, hard to find, balcony

12) Hungary

The area that is now Hungary was up for grabs for years after the Huns destroyed the Pax Romana that had prevailed there for the first several hundred years of the Common Era. The Goths, Lombards, Avars, and others all made a play for the territory that the Huns left behind. The Magyars until then were a tribe from the remote northern woods who then built an empire that effectively lasted from 895AD until 1526, enduring a Mongol assault once, and repelling it definitively the second time. They weren't so lucky against the Ottoman Turks, who held sway from 1525 until 1699. That's when the Austrian Habsburgs took over, then the dual monarchy, then the Communists, and now, a free democratic Hungary? We all hope so.

But are the people still ethnically Hungarian? Good question. Sometimes a language that once was synonymous with a race of people becomes attached to a place regardless of the ultimate disposition of the original people. It's no stranger than a Latin language next door in Romania in a sea of Slavs where Rome once ruled only a couple hundred years. Hungary has long been in the European mainstream, contributing Bartok and Liszt, tokay and goulash, and much more to the general culture. Oh yeah, and there are also some 1500 thermal springs and 450 public baths in Hungary. Now we know why the northerners settled here. The language is Hungarian (Magyar), the currency is Forint (HUF) and the calling code is +36.

guidehungary.com

BUDAPEST is the capital and largest city of Hungary and is the union of Buda and Pest on opposite sides of the Danube. Always something of an ethnic, uh... goulash, Hungary suffered heavily during WWII with its large Jewish population. Communism wasn't much better, but at least Budapest was on the front lines of resistance. The Hungarian Revolution of 1956 even brought the big bear in growling. And when the writing was on the wall, even before the Berlin Wall came down, Hungary was right there, opening the border to Austria to let East Germans push their Ladas toward West Germany.

These are happier days and Budapest just may have the most hostels of any city in the world. That's good for you, of course, since quantity usually implies quality in a free competitive market. Tourist destinations include the Chain Bridge that connects Buda with Pest across the Danube River; Buda Castle that overlooks the city from atop Buda Hill; the Parliament Building; St. Stephen's Basilica; Heroes' Square; and Central Market Hall. Then there's Pest, with its Belváros (Inner Town), containing the Town Hall (Fővárosi Tanács), the Inner Town Parish Church (Belvárosi plébániatemplom) and the Hungarian National Museum, located just outside the Belváros, the Neo-Renaissance State Opera House, the National Theatre, and the Museum of fine Arts.

www.budapest.com/

Homemade Hostel, Budapest, Teréz krt 22, Hungary;
www.homemadehostel.com/, T:0613022103, *info@homemadehostel.com;*
$20bed, Kitchen:Y, B'fast:N, WiFi:Y, Pvt. room:Y, Locker:Y, Recep:24/7;
Note: non-party, lift, luggage ok, tour desk, near metro, market, no bunks

Paprika Hostel, 1066 Budapest, Weiner Leó utca 9 1/1, Hungary;
paprikahostel.com/, T:06207735286, *book@paprikahostel.com*; $21bed,
Kitchen:Y, B'fast:Y, WiFi:Y, Pvt. room:N, Locker:Y, Recep:8a>10p;
Note: luggage ok, TV/DVD, pub crawls, coffee & tea, no sign, dinners

Budapest Centrum Hostel, Nádor St 26, Budapest, Hungary;
budapestcentrumhostel.com/, T:+36302969069; $20bed,
Kitchen:Y, B'fast:Y, WiFi:Y, Pvt. room:Y, Locker:Y, Recep:ltd;
Note: 2N min.stay, cash only, café, bike rent, free tour/travel desk

Bebop Hostel, Budapest Üllői Way 46, Hungary;

bebophostel.com/, T:0612104021, *stay@bebophostel.com*; $15bed, Kitchen:Y, B'fast:Y, WiFi:Y, Pvt. room:Y, Locker:Y, Recep:24/7;
Note: 3rd Fl, tour desk, laundry, supermarket close

Homeplus Hostel, Budapest, Balassi Bálint Street 27, Hungary; *www.homeplushostel.hu/*, T:0619502494, *info@homeplushostel.hu*; $16bed, Kitchen:Y, B'fast:N, WiFi:Y, Pvt. room:Y, Locker:Y, Recep:24/7;
Note: cash only, tour desk, luggage room, laundry, good location

Tigar Tim's Place, Budapest Teréz körút 58, Hungary; *tigertimsplace.com/*, T:06202928320, *tigertimsplace@hotmail.co.uk*; $23bed, Kitchen:Y, B'fast:N, WiFi:Y, Pvt. room:Y, Locker:Y, Recep:24/7;
Note: tour desk, luggage room, laundry, a/c, lift

Astoria City Hostel, 7th Dist. Rakoczi ut 4, 3rd Fl, Doorbell 27, Budapest; *astoriacityhostel.com/*, T:+3612661327, *staff@astoriacityhostel.com*; $16bed, Kitchen:Y, B'fast:Y, WiFi:Y, Pvt. room:Y, Locker:Y, Recep:24/7;
Note: tour desk, luggage room, laundry, cash only, central, pancakes!

Black Sheep Hostel, Budapest, Akácfa St 7, Hungary; *www.blacksheephostel.hu/*, T:06303718544, *info@blacksheephostel.hu*; $16bed, Kitchen:Y, B'fast:N, WiFi:Y, Pvt. room:Y, Locker:Y, Recep:24/7;
Note: cash, bar, free tour/info, luggage ok, laundry, central, pub crawls

Good Morning Budapest, Budapest, Bajcsy-Zsilinszky Way 49; *www.goodmorningbudapest.hu/*; T:06304869897; $16bed, Kitchen:Y, B'fast:N, WiFi:Y, Pvt. room:N, Locker:Y, Recep:ltd;
Note: cash, free tour/info, laundry, luggage ok, TV/DVD, no bunks!

LowCostel Hostel, Budapest, Hungária körút 190, Hungary; *www.lowcostelhostels.com*, T:06304571490, *info@lowcostelhostels.com*; $11bed, Kitchen:Y, B'fast:$, WiFi:Y, Pvt. room:N, Locker:Y Recep:ltd;

Note: café, bikes, tour desk, prkng, laundry, forex, not central, hard to find

Small Group Hostel, 1072 Budapest, Rákóczi Way 10, Hungary; *smallgrouphostel-budapest.hu/*, T:06302673279, $14bed, Kitchen:Y, *smallgrouphostel@gmail.com;* B'fast:N, WiFi:Y, Pvt. room:Y, Locker:Y, Recep:9a>5p; Note: lift, luggage room, laundry, central

Carpe Noctem (original), 1067 Budapest, Szobi St. 5, Hungary; *carpenoctemhostel.com/*, 06203658749, *carpenoctemhostel@hotmail.com;* $18bed, Kitchen:Y, B'fast:N, WiFi:Y, Pvt. room:N, Locker:Y, Recep:24/7;
Note: tour desk, laundry, luggage ok, parties, smoking inside, meals

Happy Holiday Hostel, Dob utca 49, Bell #17, 1st Fl, Budapest; *www.happyholidayhostel.com/*, T:+36209296911; $18bed, Kitchen:Y, B'fast:N, WiFi:Y, Pvt. room:Y, Locker:Y, Recep:>9p;
Note: free tour/info, advise arrival, no sign, laundry, res. area near ctr

I Love Budapest Hostel, 1065 Budapest, Révay St. 22, Hungary; *ilovebudapesthostel.com/*, T:0613126461, *reception@ilovebphostel.com;* $17bed, Kitchen:Y, B'fast:N, WiFi:Y, Pvt. room:N, Locker:Y, Recep:24/7;
Note: tour desk, luggage ok, laundry, a-c, by center, bars, clubs; no bunks

MetroMM Budapest, 1072 Budapest, Nagy Diófa St 19, Hungary; *metrommbudapest.hu/*, T:0617899325, *info@metrommbudapest.hu;* $14bed, Kitchen:Y, B'fast:N, WiFi:Y, Pvt. room:Y, Locker:Y, Recep:24/7;
Note: tour desk, luggage room, laundry

11th Hour Cinema Hostel, 1053 Budapest, Magyar St. 11, Hungary; *www.11thhourcinemahostel.com/*, T:0612662153; $12bed, Kitchen:Y, B'fast:N, WiFi:Y, Pvt. room:Y, Locker:Y, Recep:24/7;
Note: 2N min, bar/lounge, laundry, luggage ok, central, tea/coffee

Bazar Hostel, 1074 Budapest, Dohány Street 22, Hungary; *bazarhostel.com/*, T:06209207205, *info@bazarhostel.com*; $13bed, Kitchen:Y, B'fast:N, WiFi:Y, Pvt. room:Y, Locker:Y, Recep:24/7; Note: bar, tour desk, luggage ok, laundry, Jewish area of Pest

The Groove Hostel, 1137 Budapest, Szent István körút 16, Hungary; *www.groovehostel.hu/*, T:0617868038, *stay@groovehostel.hu;* $17bed, Kitchen:Y, B'fast:N, WiFi:Y, Pvt. room:Y, Locker:Y, Recep:24/7; Note: parking, luggage room, TV, balcony, central

Suite Central, Veres Palne 14, Door Bell 34, Budapest, Hungary; *www.suitehostel.com*, T:+3619503861, *suitehostel@yahoo.com;* $14bed, Kitchen:Y, B'fast:Y, WiFi:Y, Pvt. room:N, Locker:Y, Recep:ltd; Note: advise arrival time, free tour-travel desk, laundry, luggage ok, forex

Aventura Boutique Hostel, Visegrádi utca 12, Dist. 13, Budapest; *aventurahostelbudapest.com*, T:0612390782, *info@aventurahostel.com;* $16bed, Kitchen:Y, B'fast:$, WiFi:Y, Pvt.room:Y, Locker:Y, Recep:24-7; Note: no c.c., tour desk, laundry, luggage room, safety deposit

Bridge Hostel Budapest, 1053 Budapest, Kossuth Lajos St 14; *www.bridgehostel.eu/*, T:+36703892141; $22bed, Kitchen:Y, B'fast:$, WiFi:Y, Pvt. room:Y, Locker:Y, Recep:24/7; Note: cash only, free tour, lift, TV, central, non-party

Corvin Point Rooms/Apts., 1082 Nap utca 4, 1st Fl, VIII Dist, Budapest; *www.corvinpoint.com/*, T:+36.70.544.0224, *info@corvinpoint.com*; $17bed, Kitchen:Y, B'fast:N, WiFi:Y, Pvt. room:Y, Locker:Y, Recep:24/7;
Note: bikes, free tour, travel desk, luggage ok, laundry, forex, a/c, cc ok

Instant Groove! Party Hostel, Nagymezo u. 38, Budapest, Hungary; *www.groovehostel.hu*, T:003612694871, *instant@groovehostel.hu*; $12bed, Kitchen:Y, B'fast:N, WiFi:Y, Pvt. room:N, Locker:Y, Recep:24-7;

Note: bar/club, free tour, laundry, luggage room, a/c, club noise

Casa de la Musica Hostel, 1088 Budapest, Vas St. 16, Hungary; *casadelamusicahostel.com/*, T:06703737330, *hostel@casadelamusica.hu;* $12bed, Kitchen:Y, B'fast:N, WiFi:Y, Pvt. room:Y, Locker:Y, Recep:24-7; Note: resto/café/bar, coffee/tea, free tour/info, TV, pool, laundry, bike rent

Friends Hostel Budapest, 1066 Budapest, Teréz körút 4, Hungary; *www.friendshostel.hu/*, T:06202650578, *info@friendshostel.hu*; $15bed, Kitchen:Y, B'fast:$, WiFi:Y, Pvt. room:Y, Locker:Y, Recep:ltd; Note: resto/bar/club, forex, tour desk, laundry, luggage room, central

Interflat Youth Hostel, 1067 Budapest, Podmaniczky St. 27; *interflat.eu/*, T:0613010988, *iflat@enternet.hu*; $14bed, Kitchen:Y, B'fast:N, WiFi:Y, Pvt. room:Y, Locker:Y, Desk hr:24/7; Note: free tour, travel desk, forex, laundry, luggage room, a/c

Hostel Budapest Center, 1052 Budapest, Semmelweis utca 2; *www.hostelbudapestcenter.com/*, T:0617813364; $18bed, Kitchen:Y, B'fast:$, WiFi:Y, Pvt. room:Y, Locker:Y, Recep:24/7; Note: wheelchair ok, lift, laundry, parking, forez, c.c ok, free tour

Unity Hostel Budapest, Budapest H-1068, Kiraly utca 60, 3rd Fl; *www.unityhostel.com/*, T:(+36)14137377, *info@unityhostel.com*; $15bed, Kitchen:Y, B'fast:Y, WiFi:Y, Pvt. room:Y, Locker:Y, Recep: 24/7; Note: free tour, travel desk, lift, laundry, luggage room

Broadway Hostel, 1066 Budapest, Ó Street 24, Hungary; *www.broadwayhostel.hu/*, T:0616881662; $19bed, Kitchen:Y, B'fast:$, WiFi:Y, Pvt. room:Y, Locker:Y, Recep:24/7; Note: bike rent, parking, TV, tour desk, luggage room

Antique Guesthouse & Hostel, 1011 Budapest, Iskola St 31, Hungary; *www.antiquehostel.eu/*, T:06705800056, *info@antiquehostel.eu*; $14bed, Kitchen:Y, B'fast:$, WiFi:Y, Pvt. room:Y, Locker:N, Desk hr:ltd;

Note: vegan restaurant, tour desk, laundry

Budapest Budget Hostel, 1095 Budapest, Ipar St 15-21, Hungary; bbhostel.hu/; T:06307516055, *bpbhostel@gmail.com*; $11bed, Kitchen:Y, B'fast:N, WiFi:Y, Pvt. room:Y, Locker:Y, Recep:24/7;
Note: 2N min. stay, cash only, free tour, parking, luggage room, forex

Grandio Party Hostel, 1075 Budapest, Nagy Diófa St 8, Hungary; *grandiopartyhostel.com/*,T:06203507441, *grandiopartyhostel@gmail.com;* $8bed, Kitchen:N, B'fast:N, WiFi:Y, Pvt. room:N, Locker:Y, Recep:24/7;
Note: bar/club, tour desk, luggage room, bike rent, pub crawls

Adagio Hostel, Erzsébet körút 25-27, 2nd Fl. 9. Doorbell:15, Budapest; *www.adagiohostel.com*, T:+3619514138, *adagiohostel@gmail.com*; $13bed, Kitchen:Y, B'fast:$, WiFi:Y, Pvt. room:Y, Locker:Y, Recep:24/7;
Note: lift, café, forex, free tour/info, laundry, some rooms w/o windows

Casa Nostra, Ráday St 31J, Dist.9, 2nd Fl, left balcony; bell 47, Budapest; *casahostel.com/*, T:06204040222, *reservation@casahostel.com;* $20bed, Kitchen:Y, B'fast:$, WiFi:Y, Pvt. room:Y, Locker:Y, Recep:24/7;
Note: anti-party, resto/bar, parking, free tour, travel desk, wheelchair ok

Baroque Hostel, 1071 Budapest, Dózsa György utca 80/a, Hungary; *www.baroquehostel.hu/*, T/F:+3617883718, *info@baroquehostel.hu;* $16bed, Kitchen:Y, B'fast:N, WiFi:Y, Pvt.room:Y, Locker:Y, Recep:24-7;
Note: bike rent, parking tour desk, laundry, luggage room

Marco Polo Top Hostel, 1072 Budapest, Nyár Street 6, Hungary; *www.marcopolohostel.com/*, T:0614132555, *sales@marcopolohostel.com;* $18bed, Kitchen:Y, B'fast:$, WiFi:Y, Pvt. room:Y, Locker:Y, Recep:24/7;
Note: resto/bar, tour desk, laundry, luggage room, c.c. ok, central, cozy

Hostel Relax, Láncszem u.10, Budapest, Hungary 1183; *hostelrelax.hu/*, T:0036203216883, *info@hostelrelax.hu;* $10bed, Kitchen:Y, B'fast:N, WiFi:Y, Pvt. room:Y, Locker:N, Recep:ltd; Note: luggage ok, laundry, parking, tour desk, near airport, far

Gingko Hostel, Szép u. 5, doorbell 10, Budapest, Hungary 1053; *www.ginkgo.hu/*, T:+3612666107, *info@ginkgo.hu;* $12bed, Kitchen:Y, B'fast:$, WiFi:Y, Pvt. room:Y, Locker:Y, Desk hr:24/7; Note: cash only, luggage room, laundry, tour desk

Grand Hostel, 1021 Budapest, Hűvösvölgyi út 69, Hungary; *www.grandhostel.hu/*, T:0612741111, *info@grandhostel.hu;* $12bed, Kitchen:N, B'fast:$, WiFi:Y, Pvt. room:Y, Locker:N, Recep:24/7; Note: in Buda, café/bar, bikes, tour desk, not central, laundry, parking

Locomotive Light Hostel, 1082 Budapest, Baross Tér 2, Hungary; *www.locomotive-hostel-budapest.com/*, T:06309547851; $14bed, Kitchen:Y, B'fast:N, WiFi:Y, Pvt. room:Y, Locker:Y, Recep:24/7; Note: luggage room, laundry, tour desk, bike rental, near train, TV

Backpackers Guesthouse, 1113 Budapest, Takács Menyhért St 33; *www.backpackbudapest.hu/*, 0613858946, *backpackguest@hotmail.com;* $13bed, Kitchen:Y, B'fast:N, WiFi:Y, Pvt. room:N, Locker:Y, Recep:24/7;
Note: bar, parking, tour desk, luggage room, laundry, c.c. ok

Budapest Hostel, Könyves K. krt 64, 1086 Budapest, **Hungary;** *www.hihostels.com*, T:3612100816, *sales@budapestyouthhostel.hu;* $18bed, Kitchen:N, B'fast:$, WiFi:Y, Pvt. room:Y, Locker:Y, Recep:24/7;
Note: wheelchair ok, luggage room, laundry, parking, a/c, close to bus

Eitan's Guesthouse, Teréz körút 4, Budapest, Hungary 1066; *www.eitansguesthouse.hu/*, T:(36)309541472, *eitan@mail.datanet.hu;* $15bed, Kitchen:Y, B'fast:Y, WiFi:Y, Pvt.room:Y, Locker:Y, Recep:24.7; Note: cash only, lift, luggage room, tour desk, forex, a/c, central

AGE Budapest Youth Center, 16 Ráday utca, Budapest, 1092; *www.iuventa.hu/age/*, T:+36(30)6385948, *agebudapest@gmail.com;* $14bed, Kitchen:Y, B'fast:N, WiFi:N, Pvt. room:Y, Locker:Y, Recep:ltd; Note: 3rd Fl no lift, advise arrival time, non-party, hard to find, parking

1st Apartments & Hotel, Budapest, Sip 5, Hungary; *www.1sthostel.com/*, T:06209151039, *hotelfirst@yahoo.com*; $14bed, Kitchen:Y, B'fast:N, WiFi:N, Pvt. room:Y, Locker:Y, Recep:ltd; Note: center, close to Astoria Metro

Ace Hostel, Vaci utca 46, Budapest, Hungary 1056; *www.acehostel.com/*, T:0036205885556, *fivestars@freemail.hu;* $27bed, Kitchen:Y, B'fast:N, WiFi:Y, Pvt. room:Y, Locker:N, Recep:>10p; Note: cash only, laundry, parking, advise arrival time, TV

All-Central Hostel, Bécsi St 2, Budapest, Hungary 1052; *www.allcentral.hu*, T:+3613280955, *info@allcentral.hu*; $13bed, Kitchen:Y, B'fast:$, WiFi:Y, Pvt. room:Y, Locker:Y, Recep:24/7; Note: cash, wh/chair ok, bar, luggage ok, laundry, tour desk, central

KESZTHELY is a small city on the western end of Lake Balaton, one of central Europe's largest lakes. Nearby Hevis is famous for its spas. Keszthely is easily accessible from both Budapest and Vienna.

www.keszthely.hu/en

Ambient Hostel/G.H., Vendégház és Kávéház, Sopron u.10 Keszthely; *keszthely.szallas@gmail.com*, T:+36304603536; $18bed, Kitchen:Y, B'fast:N, WiFi:Y, Pvt. room:Y, Locker:N, Recep:8a>10p; Note: advise arrival hr., TV, luggage ok, laundry, wh/chair ok, parking

PECS is located close to the border with Croatia, and has always been a religious center as well as a trade and crafts center, and more recently a center of coal mining. The city was founded by the Romans in the 2nd century and, after long being referred to as *Quinque Basilicae* ("Five Churches"), the episcopate was founded in 1009. The Ottomans conquered Pecs in 1526; the name Pecs is Turkish for "five." For over a hundred years Pecs was an

Ottoman city in classic style—mosques, baths and minarets, etc.—remnants of which still survive today and are prime tourist destinations. The mosque is now a Roman Catholic church. Other sights include the world heritage 4th C. Christian necropolis of Sopianae. The mines have closed.

en.pecs.hu/

Nap Hostel Pecs, Pécs, Király utca 23-25, 7621 Hungary; *www.naphostel.com*, T:+3672950684, *info@naphostel.com;* $13bed, Kitchen:Y, B'fast:N, WiFi:Y, Pvt. room:Y, Locker:N, Recep:24/7; Note: bar, travel desk, luggage room, laundry, coffee & tea, central

Ecohun, Petofi Sándor út 71, Kiskassa, near Pécs, Hungary 7767; *www.ecohun.com*, T:+3672377063, *durant.eva@gmail.com;* $10bed, Kitchen:Y, B'fast:Y, WiFi:Y, Pvt. room:Y, Locker:N, Recep:24/7; Note: parking, luggage room, laundry, organic farm, no bunks

REVFULOP is a town on the northern shore of Lake Balaton and the starting point for an annual swimming race across the lake. Tourism and viticulture are the big industries. The historical downtown and port are major attractions.

www.revfulop.hu/

Hullam Hostel, 8253 Révfülöp Füredi út 6. Magyarország, Hungary; *www.balatonhostel.hu/*, T:0687463089, *info@balatonhostel.hu;* $16bed, Kitchen:Y, B'fast:N, WiFi:Y, Pvt. room:Y, Locker:N, Recep:24/7;Note: bar, parking, luggage room, laundry, tour desk, goulash!

13) Kosovo

Kosovo is a mess. Once the Roman province of Dardania, it became part of the medieval Serbian Empire, which withdrew after losing the Battle of Kosovo to the Ottoman Turks in 1389. Still they never forgot, and always claimed it as their cradle of the culture. Albanians claim their ancestors were here even before all that, and regardless, they greatly outnumbered the Serbs at the time of the fall of Ottoman Turkey, precise reconstructions of the past being tricky business, what with the fog of memory and all. So when Slobodan Milosevic moved to limit Kosovo's autonomy, tempers flared. Following the Bosnian War in the 1990's, the Kosovo question was left unaddressed, so they duked it out. By this time, of course, NATO was in no mood for Serb atrocities, so they bombed Belgrade and proceeded to administer Kosovo, which declared independence in 2008. That's the way it stands to this day. Euro is the best currency to have. Serbo-Croatian and Albanian—and English—are the best languages to know. Calling code? Yeah, right…

www.visitkosova.org/

PRISTINA is the capital and largest city of the mess called Kosovo. It is rapidly rebuilding after much destruction in the Kosovo war, mostly in the modern style. Fortunately not all of the old style was obliterated. These are the best English-speakers between the UK and the UAE (thank you, NATO), and the food is good, and it's cheap. Serbs think it's still theirs. Say hey to the Professor for me. "Show me a former war zone and I'll show you a travel bargain."—H. Karges

www.virtualtourist.com/travel/Europe/Republic_of_Serbia/Pristina

Velania Guest House, Velania 4/34, Pristina, Kosovo 10000; *www.guesthouse-ks.net/*, T:038531742, *info@guesthouse-ks.net*; $13bed, Kitchen:Y, B'fast:N, WiFi:Y, Pvt. room:Y, Locker:N, Recep:24/7; Note: laundry, luggage ok, parking, coffee/tea, in the 'burbs, hard to find

14) Latvia

Latvia is one of the three Baltic States, the middle one in fact, the others being Lithuania, with which it has been intimately related since time immemorial, and Estonia, which is more closely related to non-Indo/European Finland, unlike the majority of European nations. The three Baltic countries were the last of the modern states to join European civilization. The forebears of today's Latvians traded amber with the rest of Europe since antiquity, but weren't converted to Christianity until the 13th century, by force of the Teutonic Knights (What? You didn't know that Latvia was a Crusader state?). Inclusion in the Hanseatic League quickly followed.

Borders and alliances came and went—with Poland, Lithuania, Sweden, and Russia—until Latvia was forced to join the USSR at the point of a (very large) gun in 1940, along with the other two Baltic states, the last constituent republics of that empire to "join." It was brutal, of course, and Latvia was among the first to demand reconsideration during the period of *glasnost*. Full independence came in 1991. The problem of citizenship status for a large Russian minority has yet to be resolved. Latvia is rich in flora and fauna and is environmentally aware. Hundreds of former Soviet collective farms have been converted into eco-farms. Latvian is the language; *lats* (LVL) is the currency; the phone code is +371.

www.latvia.travel/en

LIEPAJA is on the Baltic Sea and is Latvia's third largest city. It has gradually completed a transition from a military city to a modern port. There are beaches, historic architecture, and a secret military camp now open to the public.

www.latvia.travel/en/liepaja

Travellers Beach Hostel, Republikas Iela 25 (corner w/ Uliha) LV; *www.hihostels.com*, T:37128690106, *liepaja@hostel.lv;* $15bed, Kitchen:Y, B'fast:N, WiFi:Y, Pvt. room:Y, Locker:Y, Recep:24/7;
Note: bar, parking, tour desk c.c. ok, luggage room, laundry

RIGA is the largest of the Baltic capitals and a member of the Hanseatic League from the 13th century. As such it had a large resident German population and German language until 1891. It was even a Swedish city for almost a hundred years, from 1625-1710, when Peter the Great besieged Riga and won. By the time that Russia gained influence, a national awakening occurred also, and a struggle between Russia and Germany was matched by a stuggle for Latvian identity and language dominance. WWII was bad, with concentration camps and so forth, and so was Communism, with Russians occupying all positions within the country. They still haven't left, not all of them, anyway. With the arrival of budget airlines Riga is now well-connected to the rest of Europe and tourism is on the rise. The historic center is the main attraction, including the castle on the waterfront, the Doma Cathedral, and several medieval houses. It was designated a UNESCO World Heritage site.

www.latvia.travel/en/riga

Cinnamon Sally Backpacker's House, Merķeļa iela 1, Riga, LV-1050; *www.cinnamonsally.com/*, T:22042280, *ieva@cinnamonsally.com*,$13bed, Kitchen:Y, B'fast:N, WiFi:Y, Pvt. room:Y, Locker:Y, Recep:24/7;
Note: wheelchair ok, bar, laundry, luggage room, a/c, c.c. ok

Blue Cow Backpackers, Torņa iela 4, Riga, LV-1050, Latvia; *www.bluecowhostel.com/*, T:27736700, *info@bluecowbarracks.com*; $23bed, Kitchen:Y, B'fast:N, WiFi:Y, Pvt. room:Y, Locker:Y, Recep:24/7;
Note: printer, bar, TV, luggage ok, laundry, free tour/info, a/c, central

Naughty Squirrel Backpackers, Kalēju iela 50, Riga, LV-1050, Latvia; *thenaughtysquirrel.com/*, T:67220073, *info@thenaughtysquirrel.com*; $19bed, Kitchen:Y, B'fast:N, WiFi:Y, Pvt. room:Y, Locker:Y, Recep:24/7;
Note: bar, TV, free tour/info, laundry, luggage room, c.c. ok, central

Funky Hostel, 25 Krisjana Barona St, Riga, Latvia; *www.funkyhostel.com*, T:+37129105939, *funky@hostel.lv*; $21bed, Kitchen:Y, B'fast:Y, WiFi:Y, Pvt. room:Y, Locker:Y, Recep:24/7;
Note: bar, travel desk, laundry, luggage room, c.c. ok, 4th Fl, central

RedNose Hostel, Jana Street 14, Old Town, Riga, Latvia 1050; *www.rednose.lv/*, T:+37127721414, *info@rednose*; $19bed, Kitchen:Y, B'fast:$, WiFi:Y, Pvt. room:Y, Locker:Y, Recep:24/7;
Note: parking, c.c. ok, central

Riga Style Hostel, Alfrēda Kalniņa Street 4-11, *Riga*, LV-1010; *rigastylehostel.com/*, T:+37167280830, *info@rigastylehostel.com*; $13bed, Kitchen:Y, B'fast:$, WiFi:Y, Pvt. room:Y, Locker:Y, Recep:24/7;
Note: TV, travel desk, 4th Fl no lift, c.c. ok, near train/bus/old town

Central Hostel, Ernesta Birznieka-Upīša iela 20, Riga, LV-1050, *www.centralhostel.lv/*, T:22322663, *reception@centralhostel.lv*; $7bed, Kitchen:Y, B'fast:Y, WiFi:Y, Pvt. room:Y, Locker:N, Desk hr: 24/7;
Note: laundry, luggage room, tour desk, parking, central

Domc Pearl Hostel, Tirgoņu iela 4 Riga, LV-1050, Latvia; *www.dome-hostel.com*, T:67212161, *info@hostelwelcome.com*; $16bed, Kitchen:Y, B'fast:N, WiFi:Y, Pvt. room:Y, Locker:Y, Recep:24/7;
Note: luggage room, coffee & tea, central

Riga Old Town Hostel/Backpackers Pub, Vaļņu iela 43 Riga, LV-1050; *www.rigaoldtownhostel.lv*, T:67223406, *info@rigaoldtownhostel.lv*; $12bed, Kitchen:Y, B'fast:N, WiFi:Y, Pvt. room:Y, Locker:N, Recep:24/7;
Note: café/bar, free tour, safe dep., laundry, luggage ok, c.c. ok, central

Best Hostel, Aleksandra Čaka iela 52, Riga, LV-1011, Latvia; *www.besthostel.lv/*, T:67314234, *info@besthostel.lv;* $12bed, Kitchen:N, B'fast:N, WiFi:Y, Pvt. room:Y, Locker:Y, Recep:24/7; Note: free tour, forex, luggage room, c.c. ok

Riga Backpackers Hostel, Marstalu st.6, Riga, Latvia LV-1050; *www.riga-backpackers.com/*, T:67229922, *info@riga-backpackers.com* $8bed, Kitchen:Y, B'fast:$, WiFi:Y, Pvt. room:Y, Locker:Y, Recep: 24/7 Note: bar, tour desk, close to central market

15) Lithuania

Lithuania is the largest of the three Baltic States. It shares much of the same history of the others, but its big claim to fame was the Grand Duchy of Lithuania and the commonwealth it shared with Poland for two centuries, before being finally dismantled and reduced to its current size, Russia grabbing most of it. So for much of the Middle Ages Lithuania was one of the largest and greatest countries in Europe, not bad for a nation that was only established in 1253, and for which Christianity clearly became national policy only upon the Grand duke's personal union with Poland in 1385. Upon full establishment of the commonwealth, Lithuania underwent a Polonization. The Great Northern War with Sweden devastated the country, then Russia's ever-increasing power eventually tore the commonwealth asunder in a full partition, and a plan for Russification became official policy. It was the first Soviet state to declare independence in 1990. Future's bright. Currency is *litas* (LTL); language is Lithuanian; phone code is +370.

www.nationsonline.org/oneworld/lithuania.htm

KAUNAS is Lithuania's second largest city and a major industrial center. Unlike Vilnius it is almost purely Lithuanian. It has many museums and parks and a historic old town, with many historic buildings, such as the ruins of the castle at the confluence of the rivers, the Vytautas Church, the Holy Trinity Church, and the Jesuit Church

visit.kaunas.lt/W3/titulinis?lang=en

R Hostel, Vytauto pr. 83-9, Kaunas 44238, Lithuania;

www.r-hostel.lt, T:(8)60123625, *r_hostel@yahoo.com*; $12bed, Kitchen:Y, B'fast:N, WiFi:Y, Pvt. room:Y, Locker:Y, Recep:24/7; Note: TV, laundry, luggage ok, parking, central, bikes, pub crawls

Hostel 10, Neries kr. 16, Kaunas, Lithuania LT-48402; *www.hostel10.lt*, T:+37037302218, *info@hostel10.lt*; $13bed, Kitchen:Y, B'fast:N, WiFi:Y, Pvt. room:N, Locker:N, Recep:24/7; Note: 30 min. walk to center, parking, a/c

VILNIUS is Lithuania's main city and capital, and a picturesque one at that. Its origins are murky but by the time of the commonwealth with Poland city walls were being built, a university opened, and migrants were coming from all over. That all changed with the Russian occupation a few centuries later. Its Jews were massacred in WWII, and its intelligentsia deported afterward. Then ordinary citizens were deported and Russians moved in, until 1991. Today it is a modern European city. Bigger than Tallinn, it is still easily walkable. The entire center is a UNESCO world heritage site. There are castles, cathedrals, genocide museums, the ruins of the Castle of Gediminas on Castle Hill, a 16th C. Gothic Church of St. Anne, a dozen 17th C. Baroque churches, notably the Church of SS. Peter and Paul, a cathedral that dates from 1387, and... a monument to Frank Zappa. It has not yet been colonized for Western parties. Give it another year or two.

www.vilnius-life.com/

Hostelgate, Sv. Mikalojaus 3, Vilnius, Lithuania; *www.hostelgate.lt/*, T:+37063832818, *hostelgate@gmail.com;* $16bed, Kitchen:Y, B'fast:N, WiFi:Y, Pvt. room:Y, Locker:Y, Recep:24/7; Note: free tour, travel desk, laundry, luggage ok, parking, c.c. ok, central

Paupio Namai, Paupio str. 31a, Vilnius, Lithuania LT-11341; *www.paupio-hostel-vilnius.com;* T:+37052643113; $20bed, Kitchen:Y, B'fast:N, WiFi:Y, Pvt. room:Y, Locker:N, Recep:24/7; Note: parking, laundry, forex, doctor/nurse on call, close to center

Old Town Hostel, Aušros Vartų gatvė 20, Vilnius LT-02100; *www.oldtownhostel.lt*, T:+37052625357, *oldtownhostel@lha.lt*; $13bed, Kitchen:Y, B'fast:N, WiFi:Y, Pvt. room:Y, Locker:N, Recep:24/7; Note: linen & towel fee, tour desk, close to station and old town

Youth Hostel Filaretai, Filaretu Street 17, Vilnius, Lithuania; *www.filaretaihostel.lt*, T:+37052154627, *info@filaretaihostel.lt*; $13bed, Kitchen:Y, B'fast:N, WiFi:Y, Pvt. room:Y, Locker:N, Recep:24/7; Note: HI member discount, laundry, c.c. ok, uphill 15 min. walk from ctr

Fortuna Hostel, Liepkalnio str. 2 Vilnius, 02103 Lithuania; *www.fortunahostel.lt/en/*, T:+37062345050; *fortunahostel@lha.lt*; $13bed, Kitchen:Y, B'fast:N, WiFi:Y, Pvt. room:Y, Locker:N, Recep:24/7; Note: free tour, travel desk, parking, luggage room, c.c. ok

A Hostel, **Sodu str. 8 and Sodu str. 17, LT- 01313, Vilnius;** *www.hostelsvilnius.lt*; **T:**(8)69909903, *info@hostelsvilnius.lt*; $11bed, Kitchen:N, B'fast:$, WiFi:Y, Pvt. room:Y, Locker:Y, Recep:24/7; Note: laundry, safe deposit, c.c. ok, very near stations, basement rooms

16) Macedonia

Better known as the ancient kingdom of Phillip II and Alexander the Great, the modern independent republic of Macedonia is the "other" component of the ex-Yugoslavia, the one that is landlocked, besides Kosovo, and somewhat different from all the rest. For one thing, it has historic connections with Greece, resulting in a naming problem for the modern country, FYROM the country like the artist formerly known as TAFKAP. For another thing, its language is more closely related to Bulgaria, with which it is mutually intelligible. Add to that a large Albanian Muslim minority, and there is potential for problems. After many years of being known as "southern Serbs," Macedonia is only now coming to grips with its own identity, which is a work in progress. It has never been independent before, and is by definition multi-ethnic, generally Slavic, mostly ethnically Bulgarian. This is the backwash of the former Yugoslavia, but that's not bad.

What with disruptions in trade in the first decade of its existence, independence has not been easy, but political resolutions have made life better the last decade and Macedonia is rapidly incorporating into Europe. Its natural beauty, cultural offerings and warm climate also make it a popular tourist destination, almost one million per year at last count. There are art, poetry and music festivals, especially in summer. It is connected by road to all its neighbors. Macedonian is the language, *denar* (MKD) is dinero, and +389 is the phone code.

http://travel2macedonia.com.mk/

SKOPJE is home to about a third of Macedonia's two million people. Following on the efforts of Neolithic tribes (mostly Illyrian), Romans, Byzantines, Bulgarians, and Serbs, the Ottoman Turks ruled here for over five hundred years, giving Skopje a distinct appearance for which it was famous. Since then it has industrialized and been hit with an earthquake, which left some 1,070 persons dead and more than 120,000 homeless. It also altered the city's appearance drastically and introduced modern architecture. Landmarks include a Byzantine fortress, an Oriental bazaar, a stone bridge and the Millennium Cross on Mt. Vodno. Then there are the Medieval monastery of Nerezi, a medieval Turkish inn, the Kuršumli Han, and several mosques. There is a healthy nightlife and festivals in the summer. Mother Teresa is the favorite daughter.

http://travel2macedonia.com.mk/tourist-attractions/skopje

Urban Hostel, Mother Teresa 22, Skopje; *www.urbanhostel.com.mk,* T:+38926142785, *contact@urbanhostel.com.mk;* $17bed, Kitchen:Y, B'fast:Y, WiFi:Y, Pvt. room:Y, Locker:Y, Desk hr:24/7;
Note: bar, laundry, luggage room forex, a/c, c.c. ok, central, coffee/tea

Shanti Hostel, Rade Jovcevski Korcagin 11, Madjir Maalo, Skopje; *www.shantihostel.com,* T:+38926090807, *hostelshanti@gmail.com;* $10bed, Kitchen:Y, B'fast:Y, WiFi:Y, Pvt. room:Y, Locker:Y, Recep:24/7;
Note: luggage room, laundry, forex, parking, a/c, near bus, walk to center

City Hostel, Str. Tome Arsovski nu.6, Skopje, Macedonia; *hostel-skopje.com/,* T:0038971447369, *info@hostel-skopje.com*; $12bed, Kitchen:Y, B'fast:Y, WiFi:Y, Pvt. room:Y, Locker:Y, Recep:ltd;
Note: bar, parking, luggage room, travel desk, c.c. ok, good location

Nice Hostel-Skopje, 11 Oktomvri 23-2-8, Skopje, Macedonia; *www.skopje-hostel.com,* T:+38971303499, *skopje.hostel@gmail.com*; $12bed, Kitchen:Y, B'fast:N, WiFi:Y, Pvt. room:Y, Locker:N, Recep:24/7;
Note: laundry, parking, forex, bike rent, a/c, good location, staff scarce

17) Moldova

The history of Moldova, also previously known as Moldavia and/or Bessarabia, is intricately intertwined with that of Romania, as there's nothing but a river separating them. They speak the same language, but Moldova used to be a part of the USSR. In fact throughout history the borders between them were fluid and shifting. As with Romania it enters history in the early centuries of the Common Era. It suffered repeated invasions and in 1538 became tributary to the Ottomans. It was ceded to the Russians in the 19th century, and the process of Russification began. Moldova alternately protested and requested help from Romania, but to no avail, and it became a Soviet Socialist Republic.

The USSR even tried to wedge the two apart, insisting that the Moldovan language be written in Cyrillic instead of the Roman alphabet. Moldova indeed was one of the first countries to break with the USSR, in spite of the fact that Big Bro Romania wasn't really any better. On the other border exists the proto-state of Transnistria consisting of majority Ukrainians and Russians with no sympathy at all toward the government of the land they continue to occupy. The Moldovans failed to thrive immediately, too, instead re-electing the same Communists in 2001 that once ruled with an iron hand. Still they inch their way toward a new future with a market economy. The wines are reportedly good. Moldovan/Romanian and Russian are the languages, currency is the *leu* (MDL) and the calling code is +373.

www.moldova.md/

CHISINAU is the principal city of Moldova and is centrally located. Originally a monastery village, most of its growth has come in the last two centuries. Thus there is little ancient architecture to enjoy viewing, but still the atmosphere is pleasant enough. There are easy road connections to Romania and Ukraine.

www.nationsonline.org/oneworld/moldova.htm

Retro Moldova Hostel, St. Cosbuc 3, Ap. 24, Chisinau, Moldova; *retromoldovahostel.webs.com/*, T:+37322227091, $15bed, Kitchen:N, B'fast:Y, WiFi:Y, Pvt. room:N, Locker:Y, Recep:24/7;
Note: free tour/info, laundry, luggage ok, new, hard to find w/o sign

Chisinau Hostel, 5/4 Arborilor St, Chisinau, Moldova; *chishinau.ucoz.com/*, **T:**+37360079998, *chishinauhostel@gmail.com*, $12bed, Kitchen:Y, B'fast:Y, WiFi:Y, Pvt. room:Y, Locker:N, Recep:24/7;
Note: forex, parking, laundry, luggage ok, tour desk, nr mall not central

Central Youth Hostel, Pruncul 6, Apt. 1, Chisinau, MD-2005; *www.luxlana.net/*, T:(0)69165529, *c_sveta@mail.ru;* $11bed, Kitchen:N, B'fast:N, WiFi:Y, Pvt. room:N, Locker:N, Recep:24/7;
Note: left luggage, forex, tour desk, share flat, hard find, central

18) Montenegro (Crna Gora)

Though it sounds more like a casino than a country, Montenegro ("Black Mountain" in any language) is in fact that small country that lies north of Albania, south of Bosnia, and west of Serbia, the last two to which it was long attached as part of Yugoslavia. Variously ruled by Romans, Byzantines, Serbs, Bulgarians, and Ottomans, before finally establishing a Montenegrin identity and polity, in the past century Montenegro was first a Kingdom, before becoming a constituent state in Yugoslavia. In fact it has an even longer history with Serbia, only having separated culturally after the fall of the Serbian Empire in the wars of the Kosovo region in the 14th century, and the changes that then there occurred under Ottoman rule. Montenegro was also the last to leave Yugoslavia, some fifteen years after most of the rest (so don't be surprised if you can't find it on older maps; it's that part of Serbia that bordered the sea).

After participating in the Croatian War of the early 1990's with Serbia, to gain Dubrovnik and the land around it, while handing Bosnian refugees over to the Serbs, Montenegro finally voted for independence in 2006. The economy has shown steady growth since then, and the coast is rapidly developing for tourism. Development so far seems to have a distinct Russian flavor to it, though, so it may be too late for the kind of Italian-flavored coast of Croatia. Selling passports to fugitive tycoons is a dubious career move, also. Montenegrin (Serbo-Croatian) is language; Euro is currency; calling code is +382.

www.discover-montenegro.com/

BUDVA is one of the oldest settlements on the Adriatic coast, with roots going back past the Roman to the Greek era. It was ruled by the Venetians during the years of the Renaissance. That is the era of the original architecture in Old Town, Budva's main tourist attraction. Unfortunately it was destroyed in the 1979 earthquake, but has since been rebuilt. The infrastructure has yet to keep up with the tourist boom, though, and millionaires are snapping up real estate and squeezing the locals out, or at least out of their fishing jobs into jobs servicing the rich. On the other hand, there was only one hostel when I visited only three years ago, so things are definitely progressing.

www.visit-montenegro.com/cities-budva.htm

Montenegro Freedom Hostel, Barjaktarska, Budva, Montenegro; *montefreedomhostel.com/*, 067523496, *montenegrofreedom@gmail.com*; $17bed, Kitchen:N, B'fast:Y, WiFi:Y, Pvt. room:N, Locker:Y, Recep:24/7;
Note: welcome drink, coffee & tea, bar, laundry, parking, a/c

MOJO Budva, 3 Vojvođanska, Budva, Montenegro; *www.mojobudva.com/*, T:+382(0)69711986; $17bed, Kitchen:Y, B'fast:Y, WiFi:Y, Pvt. room:Y, Locker:N, Recep:ltd;
Note: laundry, some rooms no windows, a/c, c.c. ok, hard find

Montenegro Hostel Budva, Vuka Karadzica12, Budva, Montenegro; *www.montenegrohostel.com/*, 069039751, *montenegrohostel@gmail.com;* $20bed, Kitchen:Y, B'fast:N, WiFi:Y, Pvt.room:Y, Locker:Y, Recep:>12m; Note: luggage room, laundry, a/c, old town, close to beach, hard to find

Saki-Apartmani, IV proleterska BB, Budva, Montenegro; *www.saki-apartmani.com*, T:067368065, *sakiadrovic@yahoo.com;* $16bed, Kitchen:N, B'fast:$, WiFi:Y, Pvt. room:Y, Locker:N, Recep:24/7;
Note: cash only, resto/bar, laundry, luggage room, hard to find

Hippo Hostel, IV Proleterska, 37, Budva, Montenegro; *www.hippohostel.com;* T:+38269256117, *info@hippohostel.com*; $20bed, Kitchen:Y, B'fast:N, WiFi:Y, Pvt. room:Y, Locker:Y, Recep:ltd;
Note: luggage room, laundry, parking, beach towels, eggs!

Hostel Adrovic, UI. IV Proleterska 39, Budva, Montenegro; *adrovic.zzl.org/*, T:+38269696029, *edomontenegro@t-com.me*; $14bed, Kitchen:Y, B'fast:N, WiFi:Y, Pvt. room:Y, Locker:Y, Recep:24/7; Note: luggage room, laundry, forex, parking, a/c, wheelchair ok

KOTOR is a world heritage site for its old town architecture, and the dramatic landscape only enhances its tourist appeal. There are the Romanesque cathedral of St. Tryphon and the Baroque church of Our Lady of the Rocks on an islet in the Bay of Kotor. Situated on the coast to the north of Budva, this is a nice alternative to the more established tourist towns, both in Montenegro and Croatia.

www.visit-montenegro.com/cities-kotor.htm

Montenegro Hostel Kotor, Pjaca od Mlijeka b.b., Kotor, Montenegro; *www.montenegrohostel.com*, 069039751, *montenegrohostel@gmail.com;* $17bed, Kitchen:Y, B'fast:$, WiFi:Y, Pvt.room:Y, Locker:Y, Recep:>12m;
Note: restaurant, travel desk, a/c, old town Kotor, laundry, good views

PODGORICA is Montenegro's capital and largest city, though at only 150,000 people it's not overwhelming. Centrally located, it is on a historic trade route through the region. If you have any official business—onward visas, etc.—this is where you come.

www.inyourpocket.com/montenegro/podgorica

Montenegro Hostel Podgorica, Djecevica 25, Podgorica, Montenegro; *www.montenegrohostel.com/*, 069039751, *montenegrohostel@gmail.com;* $20bed, Kitchen:Y, B'fast:N, WiFi:Y, Pvt.room:Y, Locker:Y, Recep:>12m; Note: parking, close to everything, smoking inside

TIVAT is yet another coastal option, lying halfway between Budva and Kotor. The big attraction here is nautical tourism—marinas and yachting clubs. There are good beaches and an ex-Club Med.

www.tivat.travel/

Hostel Anton, Mazina bb, Tivat, Tivat, Montenegro; *hostelanton.com/*, T:+38269261182, *hostel.anton09@gmail.com*; $14bed, Kitchen:N, B'fast:Y, WiFi:Y, Pvt. room:Y, Locker:N, Recep:24/7; Note: bar, laundry, parking, a/c, sea views

19) Poland

Poland has always had the unique position of being intermingled with the West and the East, with many Germans and Jews, among others, lying within its borders, borders that are flexible and changing with the tides of politics. Details are sketchy, but its origin as a state is closely identified with the adoption of Christianity in 966. It once tasted greatness starting in the 1500's in partnership with Lithuania before being decimated and deposed in 1795. It regrouped and there was a brief independence between WWI & II, before final independence with the fall of Communism in 1989. The drive to undermine Communism began right here, with Lech Walesa and the Solidarity movement in the shipyards of Gdansk. Prime tourist destinations today include Nazi concentration camps and many national parks, featuring lakes, rivers, forests, and even a desert. A desert in Poland? You heard it here first. Poland also has thirteen—count 'em—UNESCO World Heritage sites. It is truly one of the unpolished travel gems of Europe. Polish is the language; *zloty* is the currency; the phone code is +48.

www.poland.pl/

GDANSK ('Danzig' in German), on the northern Baltic coast, is Poland's largest seaport and fourth-largest city. Like Wroclaw, Gdansk also has swung back-and-forth between German and Polish overlordship. It was founded in the earliest years of the Common Era by Goths in migration, and then Slavic Pomeranians. With the arrival of Teutonic knights and the foundation of the Hanseatic League, Germans returned to a position of dominance, a situation in effect until the end of WWII, when the city was returned to Poland and German residents left. Since then Gdansk has always been a scene of unrest. This is the birthplace of Solidarity, which put the first chinks in Soviet armor that eventually led to the downfall of Communism in Europe.

Historical architecture is the main attraction today. Long Street and Long Market are the main tourist areas. The National Museum and the Maritime Museum are important, as is the Dominican Fair, which originated in 1260.

www.gdansk-life.com/

La Guitarra Hotel Gdansk, Grodzka 12, Gdansk, Poland;
www.lagitarra.com/, T:510795535, *gdansk@lagitarra.com*; $16bed,
Kitchen:Y, B'fast:Y, WiFi:Y, Pvt. room:Y, Locker:Y, Recep:24/7;
Note: coffee/tea, luggage ok, laundry, parking c.c. ok, central, new

Happy Seven Hostel, Grodzka 16, Gdańsk, Poland;
www.happyseven.com/, T:583208601, *booking@happyseven.com;* $16bed,
Kitchen:Y, B'fast:Y, WiFi:Y, Pvt. room:Y, Locker:Y, Recep:24/7;
Note: coffee/tea, bar, parking, luggage ok, tour desk, c.c. ok, shoes off

Hostel Wolna Chata, Krzywoustego 8, Gdańsk, Poland;
www.hostelwolnachata.com/, **T:**587463351, *info@hostelwolnachata.com;*
$11bed, Kitchen:Y, B'fast:Y, WiFi:Y, Pvt. room:Y, Locker:Y, Recep:ltd;
Note: parking, luggage room, bike rental, non-tourist area

Grand Hostel Gdansk, Kołodziejska 2, Gdańsk, Poland;
www.grandhostel.pl, T:666061350, *grand.hostel.gda@gmail.com;* $17bed,
Kitchen:Y, B'fast:Y, WiFi:Y, Pvt. room:Y, Locker:Y, Recep:24/7;
Note: bikes, luggage ok, laundry, a/c, c.c. ok, central, shoes off, no lift

Old Town Hostel, Długa Grobla 7, Gdańsk, Poland;
www.hostel.gda.pl/, T:583513131, *hostel@hostel.gda.pl*,; $14bed,
Kitchen:Y, B'fast:Y, WiFi:Y, Pvt. room:Y, Locker:Y, Recep:24/7;
Note: bike rent, parking, luggage room, laundry, c.c. ok, walk>center

Hostel Zappio, Świętojańska 49, Gdańsk, Poland;
www.zappio.pl/, T:583220174, *zappio@zappio.pl*; $14bed,
Kitchen:Y, B'fast:$, WiFi:Y, Pvt. room:Y, Locker:Y, Recep:24/7;
Note: bikes, bar/cafe, luggage ok, forex, c.c. ok, Sat TV, central

Lucky-Hostel, Księdza Robaka 3, Gdańsk, Poland;

www.lucky-hostel.com/, T:587762240, *lucky-hostel@lucky-hostel.com;*
$8bed, Kitchen:N, B'fast:Y, WiFi:Y, Pvt. room:Y, Locker:N, Recep:24/7;
Note: luggage ok, laundry, parking, forex, c.c. ok, bus 15 min. to center

Hostel Przy Targu Rybnym, Grodzka 21, Gdańsk, Poland;
www.gdanskhostel.com.pl, T:583015627, *gdanskhostel@hotmail.com;*
$13bed, Kitchen:Y, B'fast:Y, WiFi:Y, Pvt. room:Y, Locker:Y, Recep:24/7;
Note: coffee/tea, luggage room, laundry, parking, c.c. ok, good location

Baltic Hostel, Wałowa 52, Gdańsk, Poland;
www.baltichostel.com.pl/, T:587219657; $11bed, Kitchen:N, B'fast:Y, WiFi:Y, Pvt. room:Y, Locker:N, Desk hr:24/7;
Note: central, free soup, residents, parking, luggage room, laundry

LODZ is located in almost the exact geographic center of Poland. Once an economic boomtown based on the production of cotton textiles, it went from a village of a few hundred to a half million over the course of the 19th century. WWII was hard on Lodz, and the textile industry has gone elsewhere, but today Lodz survives and thrives as Poland's third city because of its central location and foreign investment in its manufacturing base. Though an ancient village, it is a relatively modern city, with few historical buildings. Still it is a cultural center, with The Museum of Modern Art, the Museum of Textiles, a flourishing art community and a film industry that has produced filmmakers like Andrzej Wajda and Roman Polanski.

www.lodz-online.eu/

Music Hostel, Piotrkowska 60, Łódź, Poland;
www.music-hostel.pl/, T:+48533533263, *rezerwacje@music-hostel.pl*;
$14bed, Kitchen:N, B'fast:Y, WiFi:Y, Pvt. room:Y, Locker:Y, Recep:24/7;
Note: parking, luggage room, laundry, central, hard to find 1st time

Flamingo Hotel Lodz, Henryka Sienkiewicza 67, Łódź, Poland; *www.lodz.flamingo-hostel.com/*, T:426611888, *lodz@flamingo-hostel.com;* $13bed, Kitchen:N, B'fast:Y, WiFi:Y, Pvt. room:Y, Locker:Y, Recep:24/7; Note: luggage room, c.c. ok, bike rent, no lift to top floors

LUBLIN is located far to the east and has a castle. It was a great center of Jewish scholarship for the Talmud and Kabbalah in the 1500's. Four hundred years later, the Lublin Ghetto's residents would be sent to Belzec for extermination. Labor strikes in Lublin in 1980 were an impetus for the Solidarity movement a month later. These days Lublin is a center of the IT industry. It also has several universities and many students. The poverty of the surrounding region and subsequent low wages and costs make it an attractive place of investment. There are music, art, and festivals. Landmarks include the medieval castle and the Chapel of the Holy Trinity which houses the Lublin Museum. At the concentration camp is a museum and memorial park.

www.um.lublin.eu/

Hostel Lublin, ul Lubartowska 60, Lublin, Poland; *hostellublin.pl/*, T:792888632, *poczta@hostellublin.pl;* $13bed, Kitchen:Y, B'fast:Y, WiFi:Y, Pvt. room:Y, Locker:N, Recep:24/7; Note: parking, luggage room, safety deposit, central, dodgy street

KRAKOW (pronounce 'w' as 'v') is the second largest and oldest city in Poland. It dates back to the seventh century and served as capital for most of the time since Poland's origin as a state. It was almost completely destroyed by the Mongols before being able to repel them. It was a trade city of the Hanseatic League and capital of the Polish-Lithuania Commonwealth before that entity was partitioned. After that Krakow became known as a center of art and culture and education. In the 20th century it was a center of Jewish culture and Zionism, and the city closest to Auschwitz.

Today the entire historic center is a world heritage site and the architecture here is a Renaissance monument. Besides Auschwitz, prime tourist sights include Wawel Castle and the old Jewish quarter, one of the largest in the world. Krakow had more than a hundred synagogues prior to WWII. Its architecture fared better than its Jewish population, and includes St. Mary's Church, Wawel Cathedral, The Barbican, the 13th C. Florian Gate, and Cloth Hall. Hostels are of high quality, and demand is equally high, advance payments sometimes being required in high season.

www.cracow-life.com/

Greg & Tom (Jr.) Party Hostel, Zyblikiewicza 9, Kraków, Poland;
www.gregtomhostel.com, T:124225525, *junior@gregtomhostel.com;*
$17bed, Kitchen:Y, B'fast:Y, WiFi:Y, Pvt. room:Y, Locker:Y,
Recep:24/7;
Note: age 18-40, bar, lounge, laundry, dinner, parties, TV, a/c, c.c. ok

Flamingo Hostel, Szewska 4, Kraków, Poland;
www.flamingo-hostel.com/, T:124220000, *Krakow@flamingo-hostel.com;*
$25bed, Kitchen:Y, B'fast:Y, WiFi:Y, Pvt. room:Y, Locker:Y,
Recep:24/7;
Note: restaurant, laundry, luggage room, free tour/travel info

Football Corner Hostel, Ul. Wróblewskiego 3, Kraków, Poland;
footballcorner.com.pl/, T:503764365, *footballcorner@home.pl;*
$11bed, Kitchen:Y, B'fast:Y, WiFi:Y, Pvt. room:Y, Locker:Y,
Recep:24/7;
Note: printer, tea & coffee, laundry, luggage ok, forex, c.c. ok, near train

Pink Panther's Hostel, Ul. Św Tomasza 8, 2 piętro, Kraków, Poland;
pinkpanthershostel.com/, T:124220935, *hostel@pinkpanthershostel.com;*
$14bed, Kitchen:Y, B'fast:Y, WiFi:Y, Pvt. room:Y, Locker:Y,
Recep:24/7;
Note: free tour, travel info, TV, c.c. ok, theme nights, party, central

AAE Mosquito Hostel, rynek Kleparski 4, Kraków, Poland;
www.mosquitohostel.com/, T:660926190, *info@mosquitohostel.com;*
$19bed, Kitchen:Y, B'fast:Y, WiFi:Y, Pvt. room:Y, Locker:Y,
Recep:24/7;
Note: free tour/info, laundry, luggage ok, c.c. ok, near old town, vodka

Cracow Hostel, Rynek Główny 18, Kraków, Poland; *cracowhostel.com*, T:124291106, *hostel@cracowhostel.nazwa.pl;* $13bed, Kitchen:Y, B'fast:Y, WiFi:Y, Pvt. room:Y, Locker:Y, Recep:24/7;
Note: café, lounge, travel info, TV, c.c. ok, stairs no lift, near market sq

Soul Hostel, Warszawska 20/6, Krakow, Poland; *www.soulhostel.krakow.pl*, T:126345297, *inbox@soulhostel.krakow.pl;* $14bed, Kitchen:Y, B'fast:Y, WiFi:Y, Pvt. room:N, Locker:Y, Recep:24/7;
Note: sat TV, laundry, luggage room, tour info, c.c. ok

Flower Hostel, świętego Tomasza 5, Kraków, Poland; *flowerhostel.pl/*, T:123505918, *office@flowerhostel.pl;* $17bed, Kitchen:N, B'fast:Y, WiFi:Y, Pvt. room:Y, Locker:Y, Recep:24/7;
Note: bike rent, laundry, luggage room, free tour, travel info, central

Traveller's Inn, Plac Na Groblach 8, Kraków, Poland; *www.travellersinn.pl*, T:602555753, *info@travellersinn.pl*; $14bed, Kitchen:Y, B'fast:Y, WiFi:Y, Pvt. room:Y, Locker:Y, Recep:24/7;
Note: bike rent, luggage room, laundry, advise arrival time

Mundo Hostel, Józefa Sarego 10, Kraków, Poland; *www.mundohostel.eu*, T:124226113, *info@mundohostel.eu;* $17bed, Kitchen:Y, B'fast:Y, WiFi:Y, Pvt. room:Y, Locker:N, Recep:24/7;
Note: bar, luggage room, laundry, c.c. ok, in courtyard, pancakes!

Elephant on the Moon Hostel, Ul. Białe Wzgórze 8, Kraków, Poland; *www.elephantonthemoon.com/*, T:695949604, *hostel24@hotmail.com;* $19bed, Kitchen:Y, B'fast:Y, WiFi:Y, Pvt. room:Y, Locker:Y, Recep:24/7;
Note: luggage room, laundry, TV, forex, parking, 20 min. walk to center

Deco Hostel, Mazowiecka 3A, Kraków, Poland; *www.hosteldeco.com*, T:126310745, *hostel@hosteldeco.pl;* $13bed, Kitchen:Y, B'fast:Y, WiFi:Y, Pvt. room:Y, Locker:N, Recep:24/7;

Note: free tour/info, luggage, laundry, theme room, 20 min walk>town

Mama's Hostel-Main Market Sq, Bracka 4, Kraków, Poland; *www.mamashostel.com.pl*, T:124295940, *hostel@mamashostel.com.pl;* $14bed, Kitchen:Y, B'fast:Y, WiFi:Y, Pvt. room:Y, Locker:Y, Recep:24/7;
Note: free tour, travel desk, party, luggage ok, TV, c.c. ok, off main sqare

Ars Hostel, Koletek 7 str., 31-069 Krakow, Poland; *www.arshostel.pl*, **T/F:+48124223659,** *info@krakowtravels.pl;* $13bed, Kitchen:Y, B'fast:Y, WiFi:Y, Pvt. room:Y, Locker:Y, Recep:24/7;
Note: cash only, bar, bike rent, luggage room, laundry, forex, off main sq

Atlantis Hostel, ul. Dietla 58, Kraków, Poland; *www.atlantishostel.pl*, T:124210861, *atlantis@hostel.pl;* $8bed, Kitchen:Y, B'fast:N, WiFi:Y, Pvt. room:Y, Locker:N, Recep:24/7;
Note: free tour/info, luggage room, c.c. ok, coffee/tea, central

Hostel Benedykta, Juliana Dunajewskiego 5, Kraków, Poland; *www.benedykta.pl*, T:124210285, *hostel@benedykta.pl;* $8bed, Kitchen:Y, B'fast:Y, WiFi:Y, Pvt. room:N, Locker:Y, Recep:24/7;
Note: luggage rm, laundry, forex, pets ok, 3-deck bunks, non-party

Highlife Hostel, Starowiślna 16, Kraków, Poland; *www.highlifehostel.com*, T:+48530144469, *booking@highlifehostel.com;* $12bed, Kitchen:N, B'fast:Y, WiFi:Y, Pvt. room:Y, Locker:Y, Recep:ltd;
Note: bar, parking, TV, luggage room, laundry

City Hostel, Świętego Krzyża 21, Kraków, Poland; *www.cityhostel.pl*, T:124261815, *cityhostel@cityhostel.pl;* $16bed, Kitchen:Y, B'fast:Y, WiFi:Y, Pvt. room:Y, Locker:Y, Recep:24/7;
Note: luggage room, laundry, c.c. OK, travel info, central, modern

Dizzy Daisy Hostel Krakow, ul.Pędzichów 9, Kraków, Poland; *www.krakowhostel.pl*, T:122920171, *krakow@hostel.pl;* $19bed,

Kitchen:Y, B'fast:$, WiFi:Y, Pvt. room:Y, Locker:Y, Recep:ltd;
Note: café, luggage ok, laundry, bikes, c.c. ok, no lift, central

Momotown Hostel, Miodowa 28, Kraków, Poland;
www.momotownhostel.com/, T:124296929, *info@momotownhostel.com;* $16bed, Kitchen:Y, B'fast:Y, WiFi:Y, Pvt. room:Y, Locker:Y, Recep:24/7;
Note: bar, parking, luggage ok, laundry, bikes, forex, c.c. ok, 4 Fl. no lift

Tutti Frutti Hostel, Kraków, 29 Floriańska St., Poland;
tuttifruttihostel.com/, T:+48124280028, *office@tfhostel.com*; $16bed, Kitchen:Y, B'fast:Y, WiFi:Y, Pvt. room:Y, Locker:N, Recep:24/7;
Note: bar/club, parking, free tour, travel info, party, c.c. ok, nr transport

Premium Hostel, Pomorska 2, 30-001 Kraków, Poland;
www.premiumhostel.pl, T:122922211, *premium@hostel.pl;* $8bed, Kitchen:N, B'fast:Y, WiFi:Y, Pvt. room:Y, Locker:Y, Recep:24/7;
Note: parking, tour info, luggage room, c.c. ok, 20 min. walk to town

Hostel Rynek 7, Rynek Główny 7, Kraków, Poland;
www.hostelrynek7.pl, T:607073252, *hostel@hostelrynek7.pl;* $14bed, Kitchen:Y, B'fast:Y, WiFi:Y, Pvt. room:Y, Locker:N, Recep:24/7;
Note: bar, tour desk, luggage room, c.c. ok, front of Old Square

GlobArt Hostel, Basztowa 15, Kraków, Poland;
www.globarthostel.pl, T:124300099, *globart@hostel.pl;* $13bed, Kitchen:Y, B'fast:$, WiFi:Y, Pvt. room:Y, Locker:Y, Recep:24/7;
Note: lift, laundry, luggage room, tour info, c.c. ok, central

Giraffe Hostel, 31 Krowoderska St, Krakow, Poland;
www.hostelgiraffe.com/, T:+48124300150, *info@hostelgiraffe.pl*; $14bed, Kitchen:Y, B'fast:Y, WiFi:Y, Pvt. room:Y, Locker:Y, Recep:24/7;
Note: bar/café, gym, laundry, luggage room, tour info, c.c. ok, parties

Orange Hostel, Józefa Dietla 64, Kraków, Poland;

www.orangehostel.pl/, T:124212712, *info@orangehostel.pl;* $17bed, Kitchen:Y, B'fast:Y, WiFi:Y, Pvt. room:Y, Locker:Y, Desk hr:24/7; Note: parking, tour info, luggage room, laundry, coffee/tea

POZNAN is Poland's fifth-largest city and one of its oldest. Located in the west of the country, Poznan, as elsewhere, has long had a significant number of ethnic German residents. That's only changed within the last century, though the Nazi occupation attempted a reversal. Poznan was devastated during WWII. They stubbornly resisted Communist rule here, too. Today Poznan is a trade city, as it was in the past. Old Town is the main tourist attraction. Notable landmarks include the cathedral (erected 968) and Poznań's 16th C. town hall with clock tower. Besides the National Museum there are museums of archaeology and of musical instruments.

www.poznan-life.com/

Hill Hostel, Zamkowa 1/2, Poznań, Poland; *www.hillhostel.pl*, T:618530910, *info@hillhostel.pl;* $16bed, Kitchen:Y, B'fast:Y, WiFi:Y, Pvt. room:Y, Locker:Y, Recep:24/7; Note: luggage room, tour desk, a/c, c.c ok, central

Frolic Goats Hostel, Wrocławska 16, Poznań, Poland; *frolicgoatshostel.com/*, T:618524411, *bookings@frolicgoatshostel.com;* $14bed, Kitchen:Y, B'fast:Y, WiFi:Y, Pvt. room:Y, Locker:Y, Recep:24/7; Note: advance dep., tour desk, luggage room, laundry, parking, c.c. ok

La Guitarra Hostel Poznan, Aleje Karola Marcinkowskiego 20, Poznań; *www.lagitarra.com/*, T:618522074, *poznan@lagitarra.com*; $14bed, Kitchen:Y, B'fast:Y, WiFi:Y, Pvt. room:Y, Locker:Y, Recep:24/7; Note: parking, wheelchairs ok, luggage room, tour desk, c.c. ok, central

Melange Hostel, Rybaki 4/6, Poznań, Poland; *www.melangehostel.com/*, T:507070107, *hostel@melangehostel.com;* $14bed, Kitchen:N, B'fast:Y, WiFi:Y, Pvt. room:Y, Locker:N, Recep:24/7;

Note: some rooms w/o windows, central, parking, tour desk, luggage room

Fusion Hostel & Hotel, Święty Marcin 66/72, Poznań, Poland; *www.fusionhostel.pl/*, T:618521230, *office@fusionhostel.pl;* $18bed, Kitchen:N, B'fast:Y, WiFi:Y, Pvt. room:N, Locker:Y, Recep:24/7;
Note: c.c. ok, futuristic design, convenient

Cinnamon Hostel, Gwarna 10/2, Poznan, Poland; *www.cinnamonhostel.com/*, T:618515757, *poznan@cinnamonhostel.com;* $11bed, Kitchen:Y, B'fast:Y, WiFi:Y, Pvt. room:Y, Locker:Y, Recep:24/7;
Note: tour desk, luggage room, laundry, TV, c.c. ok, close to old town

By the Way Hostel, Półwiejska 19, Poznań, Poland; *www.bythewayhostel.pl/*, T:698380473, *hostel@bythewayhostel.pl;* $14bed, Kitchen:Y, B'fast:Y, WiFi:Y, Pvt. room:Y, Locker:Y, Recep:24/7;
Note: tour desk, luggage room, laundry, TV, c.c. ok, central

TORUN is the birthplace of Nicolaus Copernicus. It is one of the oldest Polish cities, with roots going back to the Lusatian culture in 1100 BC, with a subsequent Slavonic and then Teutonic occupation that had to be terminated by force, and their castle destroyed in the Thirteen Years War. Due to the mixed Polish/German populace, the Protestant Reformation carried serious repercussions here. "Germanization" was even forced upon the populace, and Hitler annexed it outright. Poles couldn't reclaim it as their own until after WWII. Its medieval old town is a UNESCO world heritage site, and well preserved. It is built entirely of brick. Highlights of the historic city include the 13th C. Church of St. John, the ruins of a Teutonic castle and the Gothic Church of Mary.

www.torunonline.com/

Angel Hostel, Rynek Staromiejski 8, Toruń, Poland; *www.angelhostel.com/*, T:696528664, *torun.hostel@gmail.com;* $11bed, Kitchen:N, B'fast:$, WiFi:Y, Pvt. room:Y, Locker:Y, Recep:ltd;

Note: resto/bar/club, luggage room, call to check-in, absentee staff, center

Hostel Orange, Prosta 19, Toruń, Poland;
hostelorange.pl/, T:566520033, *rezerwacje.torun@hostelorange.pl;*
$9bed, Kitchen:Y, B'fast:N, WiFi:Y, Pvt. room:Y, Locker:Y, Recep:24/7;
Note: travel info, laundry, luggage room, two locations

Freedom Backpackers, Szeroka 31, Toruń, Poland;
www.freedomtorun.pl/, T:790704785, *freedom.backpackers@gmail.com;*
$13bed, Kitchen:Y, B'fast:Y, WiFi:Y, Pvt. room:Y, Locker:Y, Recep:24/7;
Note: cash only, laundry, luggage room, Sat TV, central, hard to find

WARSAW, near the center of the country, is Poland's capital and largest city. Like many of Europe's major cities, its roots go back to the beginning of the last millennium. It became capital of the Polish-Lithuanian Commonwealth and, after getting passed around between Germany and Russia, was capital of independent Poland after WWI.

Unfortunately it was 80% destroyed during WWII and hundreds of thousands of Jews were annihilated during the Warsaw Ghetto Uprising there. Another Warsaw Uprising near the end of the war resulted in most of the city's original architecture being systematically destroyed by the Nazis while Russian troops camped on the city's outskirts.

Since WWII the old town has been reconstructed to the original plan, and has the somewhat unique distinction that that reconstruction has been declared a World Heritage site in its own right. The only original medieval buildings are the Gothic St. John's Cathedral and the red-brick Barbican fortifications. Other significant structures include the Church of the Holy Cross, the Royal Castle, Belvedere Palace, the Alexander Citadel and the palace of Culture and Science, built by the Soviets. There are the National Museum and the Zachęta National Gallery of Art in addition to many specialized museums. The Saxon Gardens and Royal Baths are two of the best parks. Wianki is a traditional summer festival. There are music and film festivals also.

www.warsaw-life.com/

Hostel Krokodyl, Czapelska St. 24, Warszawa, Poland; *www.hostelkrokodyl.com*, T:+48228101118, *info@hostelkrokodyl.com;* $14bed, Kitchen:Y, B'fast:Y, WiFi:Y, Pvt. room:Y, Locker:Y, Recep:24/7;
Note: luggage room, laundry, parking, TV, c.c. ok, tram to center 20 min.

Lost & Found, Odolańska 42, Warsaw, Poland; *www.lostandfoundhostel.pl*, T:664019563, *info@lostandfoundhostel.pl;* $13bed, Kitchen:Y, B'fast:N, WiFi:Y, Pvt. room:Y, Locker:N, Desk hr:ltd;
Note: $3 towel, new, garden, res. area hard to find 1st time, family-run

New World Street Hostel, Nowy Świat St 27, Warsaw, Poland; *www.newworldst-hostel.pl/*, T:228281282, *hostel@nws-hostel.pl;* $15bed, Kitchen:N, B'fast:$, WiFi:Y, Pvt. room:Y, Locker:Y, Recep:24/7;
Note: no lift, store, c.c., near trans/old town, hard to find, club noise

Oki Doki Hostel, Plac Jana Henryka Dąbrowskiego 3, Warsaw; *okidoki.pl/*, T:224231212, *okidoki@okidoki.pl;* $17bed, Kitchen:N, B'fast:$, WiFi:Y, Pvt. room:Y, Locker:Y, Recep:24/7;
Note: bar, tour desk, luggage room, laundry, c.c. ok

Tamka Hostel, Tamka 30, Warsaw, Poland; *www.tamkahostel.com*, T:228263095, *tamka@hostel.pl;* $14bed, Kitchen:Y, B'fast:Y, WiFi:Y, Pvt. room:Y, Locker:Y, Recep:24/7;
Note: bike rent, tour desk, luggage room, laundry, c.c. ok

Old Town Hostel Kanonia, Jezuicka 2, Warsaw, Poland; *www.kanonia.pl/*, T:226350676, *hostel@kanonia.pl;* $18bed, Kitchen:Y, B'fast:$, WiFi:Y, Pvt. room:Y, Locker:Y, Recep:24/7;
Note: luggage room, laundry, c.c. ok, old town location

Nathan's Villa Hostel, Piękna 24/26, Warsaw, Poland; *www.nathansvilla.com/*, T:226222946, *warsaw@nathansvilla.com;*

$15bed, Kitchen:Y, B'fast:N, WiFi:Y, Pvt. room:Y, Locker:Y, Recep:24/7;
Note: laundry, luggage room, tour desk, c.c. ok

Camera Hostel, Jasna 22, Warsaw, Poland;
camerahostel.com/, T:228288600, *info@camerahostel.pl*; $12bed, Kitchen:Y, B'fast:Y, WiFi:Y, Pvt. room:Y, Locker:Y, Recep:24/7;
Note: luggage room, laundry, parking, lift

Hostel Witt, Emilii Plater 9/11, Warsaw, Poland;
www.hostelwitt.pl/, T:603632588; *rezerwacja@hostelwitt.pl*; $16bed, Kitchen:Y, B'fast:N, WiFi:Y, Pvt. room:Y, Locker:Y, Recep:ltd;
Note: scooter & bike rental, parking, TV, c.c. ok, nice old house

Hostel Fabryka, 11 Listopada 22, Warsaw, Poland;
www.hostelfabryka.pl/, T:515464209, *hostelfabryka@gmail.com;* $14bed, Kitchen:Y, B'fast:Y, WiFi:Y, Pvt. room:Y, Locker:Y, Recep:24/7;
Note: club, lounge, parking, luggage room, Praga club district

WROCLAW (pronounced something like "vrot swaf") is located in the southwest of Poland. Located at a central crossroads of Europe, besides Poland, Wroclaw, originally Silesian, has at various times been a member of Austria, Prussia, and Germany, and has different names in half a dozen different languages, creating today a modern city of mixed origins and cultures. Mostly it's been a swing city between the Germans and the Poles. It's always been Bohemian. The historic architecture here is a tourist attraction, a collective monument to the use of brick. Town Hall can't be missed; it's the wedding cake at the feast. Centennial Hall is a world heritage site. Other buildings of particular historical interest include the churches at Ostrów Tumski, and the Aula Leopoldina, a Baroque assembly hall at the university. There are music festivals.

www.wroclaw-life.com/

Mleczarnia Hostel, Pawła Włodkowica 5, Wrocław, Poland;
www.mleczarniahostel.pl/, 717877570, *rezerwacja@mleczarniahostel.pl;*

$13bed, Kitchen:Y, B'fast:N, WiFi:Y, Pvt. room:Y, Locker:N, Recep:24/7;
Note: resto/bar/café, pets ok, luggage room, laundry, c.c. ok, in old town

Boogie Hostel Wroclaw, Ruska 35, Wrocław, Poland;
boogiehostel.com/en/, T:713424472, *hostel@boogiehostel.com;* $12bed, Kitchen:Y, B'fast:Y, WiFi:Y, Pvt. room:Y, Locker:Y, Recep:24/7;
Note: tour desk, luggage room, laundry, c.c. ok, close to center

Babel Hostel, Księdza Hugona Kołłątaja 16/3, Wrocław, Poland;
babelhostel.pl/, T:694896921; *rezerwacje@babelhostel.pl;* $14bed, Kitchen:Y, B'fast:N, WiFi:Y, Pvt. room:N, Locker:Y, Recep:24/7;
Note: free tour, luggage room, laundry, TV

Kolor Hostel, Kuźnicza 56, Wrocław, Poland;
www.en.kolorhostel.pl, T:713423215, *kolor@kolorhostel.pl*; $11bed, Kitchen:Y, B'fast:N, WiFi:Y, Pvt. room:Y, Locker:N, Recep:24/7;
Note: luggage room, laundry, c.c. ok, 3 Fl. no lift, central;

Absynt Hostel, świętego Antoniego 15, Wrocław, Poland;
www.absynthostel.pl/, T:713444469, *biuro@absynthostel.pl;* $13bed, Kitchen:Y, B'fast:N, WiFi:Y, Pvt. room:Y, Locker:N, Recep:24/7;
Note: lift, tour desk, a/c, c.c. ok

Hostel Cinema, Kazimierza Wielkiego 17, Wrocław, Poland;
hostelcinema.pl/, T:717957755, *hostelcinema@o2.pl;* $13bed, Kitchen:Y, B'fast:N, WiFi:Y, Pvt. room:Y, Locker:N, Recep:24/7;
Note: coffee/tea, luggage ok, laundry, c.c ok, disco music, central

Cinnamon Hostel, Kazimierza Wielkiego 67, Wrocław, Poland;
www.cinnamonhostel.com/, T:713445858, *wroclaw@cinnamonhostel.com;* $11bed, Kitchen:Y, B'fast:Y, WiFi:Y, Pvt. room:Y, Locker:N, Recep:24/7;
Note: tour desk, luggage ok, laundry, c.c. ok, central, checkout 12, bikes

Centrum Hostel, Świętego Mikołaja 16/17, Wrocław, Poland;
www.centrumhostel.pl, T:717930870, *hostelcentrum@o2.pl;* $13bed,

Kitchen:Y, B'fast:N, WiFi:Y, Pvt. room:Y, Locker:N, Recep:24/7;
Note: confirm res. 1 day B4, central, laundry, safe deposit, c.c. ok

Hostel Europa, Ul. Grabiszynska 61-65, Wroclaw, Poland;
www.hosteleuropa.pl T:+48713437024; $11bed, Kitchen:Y,
B'fast:$, WiFi:Y, Pvt. room:Y, Locker:N, Recep:24/7;
Note: club, parking, luggage room, 15 min. walk to center

Corner Hostel, Świdnicka 13, Wrocław, Poland;
hostel-centrum.wroclaw.pl/, T:713441095, *wroclaw@cornerhostel.com;*
$11bed, Kitchen:Y, B'fast:Y, WiFi:Y, Pvt. room:Y, Locker:Y,
Recep:24/7;
Note: café, wheelchair ok, pets ok, parking, luggage room, a/c, c.c. ok

ZAKOPANE lies at the southernmost tip of Poland, where it pokes into the hilly border of Slovakia, at an elevation of some 1000m/4000ft. A former mining town, today it is a center of winter sports in the winter and a hikers' mecca in the summer. Zakopane also serves as the cultural centre for the area, with the Chałubiński Memorial Tatra Museum, containing ethnographic and geologic displays, and the Exhibition Hall of the Union of Polish Arts.

www.zakopane-life.com/

Goodbye Lenin Hostel, Chłabówka 44, Zakopane, Poland;
www.zakopane.goodbyelenin.pl/ T:182001330; $11bed,
Kitchen:Y, B'fast:Y, WiFi:Y, Pvt. room:Y, Locker:Y, Recep:24/7;
Note: prkng, luggage ok, laundry, c.c. ok, natl. park, 40 min>town

Target Hostel, Henryka Sienkiewicza 3b, Zakopane, Poland;
www.targethostel.pl/, T:182074596, *kontakt@targethostel.pl;* $10bed,
Kitchen:Y, B'fast:N, WiFi:Y, Pvt. room:N, Locker:Y, Recep:24/7;
Note: parking, laundry, luggage room, close to bus & Tesco, quiet

Flamingo Hostel Zakopane, Krupówki 24, 34-500,
zakopane.flamingo-hostel.com/, T:182000222, *zakopane@flamingo-hostel.com;*
$10bed, Kitchen:Y, B'fast:$, WiFi:Y, Pvt.room:Y, Locker:Y, Recep:24.7;
Note: parking, tour desk, laundry, luggage rm, c.c. ok, balcony over st.

Hostel Stara Polana, ul. Nowotarska 59, Zakopane, Poland; *www.starapolana.pl/*, T:182068902, *rezerwacje@starapolana.pl*; $13bed, Kitchen:Y, B'fast:Y, WiFi:Y, Pvt. room:Y, Locker:Y, Recep:24/7; Note: parking, tour desk, luggage room, laundry

20) Romania

What do you get when you take a province 2000 years ago extending from the Black Sea and beyond the Carpathians, populate them with ancient East European tribes, colonize with ancient Romans for a couple hundred years, import other tribes to work the gold and silver mines, impose Latin as the *lingua franca,* beat lightly to mix, allow to settle, penetrate with Goths, Huns, Avars, Bulgars, Pechenegs, and others, then include as side-dishes in successive Ottoman, Habsburg, and Austria-Hungarian Empires, fight a World War, allow a couple decades of independence, fight another war, become Communist in a paranoid egomaniacal police state, before finally emerging toward the end of the second millennium as a modern European country (garnish to taste)? It might look a lot like Romania, successor to a remote Roman colony almost two thousand years ago, and still speaking a form of the language, far removed from its cultural kin far to the west.

The persistence of a vast East European peasantry who considered themselves citizens of Rome, and spoke a variety of Latin, with little or no contact with the great highly civilized Latin countries of the West is one of the great anomalies of history. It is also a great lesson to anthropolinguists, especially considering that their language is probably closer to the original Latin than is French, and was colonized only a relatively brief two hundred years. The Romanian language is not even attested before the 1500's and no literature was written in the language before the 1800's. Feudalism persisted until the 1700's. Romania wasn't even a country until 1862 with the union of Wallachia and Moldavia.

History is not always written by the powerful. Even the tourist sites in Romania tend to be focused on nature—rural-based and folk-oriented. Few of the names would you recognize, but your knowledge of Europe would be incomplete without a visit to Romania. Romanian is the language; *leu* is currency; calling code is +40.

www.romaniatourism.com/

BRASOV is a city in the Transylvania region of Romania west of the Carpathians. Saxons were invited in during the 12th century to settle Transylvania and Teutonic knights to protect that region of then-Hungary. They built the "crown city" of Brasov, and the descendants of many of those settlers stayed on. Then the 19th century saw an influx of Hungarians. Romanians have had to struggle hard for equal rights throughout their history in Brasov. Most Germans were deported at the end of WWII and Romania became Communist. Now it is an all-season tourist center with winter sports and "Dracula's Castle." The old town contains many historic buildings, including the town hall, the watchtower (also called Trumpeter's Tower), the Orthodox St. Nicholas' Church, the Gothic Protestant Church and St. Bartholomew's Church, which dates from the 13th century, the oldest building in Braşov.

www.romaniatourism.com/brasov.html

Boemia Hostel, Strada George Bariţiu, Brasov, Romania; *www.hostel-boemia.com/*, T:0722275066; $14bed, Kitchen:Y, B'fast:Y, WiFi:Y, Pvt. room:N, Locker:Y, Recep:24/7;
Note: luggage room, tour desk, TV, ham & eggs, central

Jugendstube Hostel, 13 Michael Weiss St Apt 5, Brasov, Romania; *www.jugendstube.ro/*, T:+40(0)742136660, *office@jugendstube.ro;* $16bed, Kitchen:Y, B'fast:Y, WiFi:Y, Pvt. room:Y, Locker:Y, Recep:24/7;
Note: luggage room, laundry, free tour/info, coffee/tea, eggs, central

Old Town Brasov Hostel, 39 Prundului Street, Brasov, Romania; *oldtownbrasov.com/*, T:+40743434509, *office@oldtownbrasov.com;* $15bed, Kitchen:Y, B'fast:Y, WiFi:Y, Pvt. room:Y, Locker:Y, Recep:24/7;
Note: café, luggage room, laundry, parking, TV

Rolling Stone Hostel, Strada Piatra Mare 2A, Braşov, Romania; *www.rollingstone.ro*/, T:0268513965, *office@rollingstone.ro;* $11bed,

Kitchen:Y, B'fast:Y, WiFi:Y, Pvt. room:Y, Locker:Y, Recep:24/7;
Note: luggage room, laundry, bike rent, forex, parking

BUCHAREST is the capital and largest city of Romania, and a fairly modern one at that, documented from only around 1500. It became capital of Walachia in 1659, under Ottoman suzerainty, after which it grew rapidly. In 1862 it became capital of Romania, and even got some press as the "Little Paris (*Micul Paris*)" around that time, but I wouldn't go that far. It takes more than an *Arcul de Triumf* to call yourself Paris. Nevertheless the city is pleasant enough, certainly not deserving of some of the putdowns I've heard from backpackers.

Landmarks include the House of the People (Casa Poporului), Creţulescu Church, Revolution Square (formerly Palace Square), the Romanian Athenaeum, the former royal palace (now the National Art Museum), Curtea Veche (Old Court) church, the church of the former Antim Monastery (1715) and Stavropoleos church (1724). There are the Museum of the History of the City of Bucharest, the Art Museum of Romania, and the Village Museum, made up of peasant houses brought from various parts of the country. That's enlightened, because the best of Romania is in the small towns and countryside. Hostels are decent, though few have websites. I've found you those that do.

www.romaniatourism.com/bucharest.html

Hostel Tina, Odobesti 2b, Bloc N3B, 9 Fl, Ap. 38, Dist 3 i/com 38C;
www.hosteltina.com, T:0314015964, *cparpala@yahoo.com*; $17bed,
Kitchen:N, B'fast:Y, WiFi:Y, Pvt. room:Y, Locker:Y, Recep:ltd;
Note: lift, laundry, advise arrival time, printer, coffee & tea, no sign

Doors Hostel, Olimpului Street No 13, Bucharest, Romania;
doorshostel.com/, T:+40213362127, *office@doorshostel.com*; $15bed,
Kitchen:Y, B'fast:Y, WiFi:Y, Pvt. room:Y, Locker:Y, Recep:24/7;
Note: parking, tour desk, laundry, luggage room, hard to find

Happy Hostel, Street Drumea Radulescu No.32, Bucharest, Romania;
www.cazare-happyhostel.ro/, T:0769642779, *happyhostel@ymail.com;*

$13bed, Kitchen:Y, B'fast:N, WiFi:Y Pvt. room:Y, Locker:N, Recep:24/7;
Note: luggage room, laundry, tour desk, parking, c.c. ok, central

Hostel Byzanthin, Dr. Caracas Constantin, #22 St, Bucharest, Romania; *www.hostel-byzanthin.ro/*, T:+40786606097, *byzanthin@yahoo.com;*
$14bed, Kitchen:N, B'fast:Y, WiFi:Y, Pvt. room:Y, Locker:N, Recep:ltd;
Note: homestay, central

Vila Gabriela, Str.Margaritarului 18, Vila A 104, Otopeni, Judet Ilfov; *www.vilagabriela.com*, T:+40213522053, *pensiuneagabriela@yahoo.com;*
$20bed, Kitchen:Y, B'fast:Y, WiFi:Y, Pvt. room:Y, Locker:N, Recep:24/7;
Note: luggage ok, laundry, tour desk, parking, discount for HI, near arpt.

Butterfly Villa Hostel, Stirbei Voda 96, off St. C. Stahi, Bucharest; *www.villabutterfly.com*, T:0213147595, *booking@butterfly-villa.com*;
$14bed, Kitchen:Y, B'fast:Y, WiFi:Y, Pvt. room:Y, Locker:N, Recep:24/7;
Note: discount HI/YHA, luggage ok, prkng, tour desk, forex, a/c, central

Funky Chicken Hostel, St. General H.M. Berthelot 63, Bucharest; *www.funkychickenhostel.com/*, T:0213121425; $8bed, Kitchen:Y, B'fast:N, WiFi:Y, Pvt. room:Y, Locker:N, Recep:24/7;
Note: luggage room, laundry, tour desk, TV, central

Wonderland Hostel, Strada Coltei 48, Bucuresti, Romania; *www.sapteseri.ro/*, T:(+4)0729199393, *hostelwonderland@gmail.com*;
$13bed, Kitchen:N, B'fast:N, WiFi:N, Pvt. room:Y, Locker:N, Recep:>4a;
Note: bar/club, parking, luggage room, laundry, a/c, central, hard to find

CLUJ NAPOCA is Romania's second city and the unofficial capital of Transylvania. It was first documented in 1213 in Latin and shortly after in various other languages. The early village was Hungarian and Saxons were invited to settle. With them came crafts guilds and increased prosperity. When Ottoman Turks occupied Hungary, Cluj (Klausenberg) assumed a prominent place in independent Transylvania and Europe, too. Not until the end of WWI was Transylvania united with Romania and the process of Romanization begun. Until then, Romanians had been third-class citizens, after Hungarians and Saxons. Hungarians in fact were the majority ethnicity here until fifty years ago. The Germans occupied Cluj in WWII and 16,000 Jews were sent to Auschwitz. After the war came years of Communism until the revolution of 1989 and eventual democracy.

Today the economy is active after a shaky capitalist start. It may not be as romantic as some of the Carpathian towns, but it is poised for greatness. Right now that means leadership in the high-tech field. As long as that means programming and not hacking, here's wishing them luck. And then there's tourism, with abundant sights and sounds for a traveler's enjoyment, such as: the house in which Matthias I Corvinus (king of Hungary, 1458–90) was born; the Roman Catholic cathedral of St. Michael; the Bánffy Palace, now a fine arts museum; botanical gardens; a 14th C. Gothic church; an Orthodox cathedral; an ethnographic museum; castles in the countryside; music and nightlife; festivals, too.

www.romaniatourism.com/cluj.html

Hostel Transylvania, Luliu Maniu 26, First Floor, Cluj-Napoca; *www.hostelcluj.com/*, T:+40264443266, *transylvaniahostel@yahoo.com*; $15bed, Kitchen:Y, B'fast:N, WiFi:Y, Pvt. room:Y, Locker:Y, Recep:24/7;
Note: luggage room, tour desk, c.c. ok, central

Retro Hostel, Potaissa St.11-13, Cluj - Napoca, Romania; *www.retro.ro/*, T:0040264450452, *retro@retro.ro*; $13bed, Kitchen:Y, B'fast:$, WiFi:Y, Pvt. room:Y, Locker:Y, Recep:24/7;
Note: luggage room, laundry, tour desk, c.c. ok

City Center Hostel, Strada Ion Ratiu 2, Cluj-Napoca, Romania; *www.xpert.ro/*, T:0264594454, *reservari@citycenterhostel.ro*; $13bed, Kitchen:N, B'fast:$, WiFi:Y, Pvt. room:Y, Locker:Y, Recep:24/7;

Note: resto/bar, luggage room, laundry, a/c, c.c. ok

CONSTANTA, located on the Black Sea, is one of Romania's largest cities and **the** oldest, being documented from 600BC. At that time it was a Greek city, before passing to the Romans. After that it belonged to the Bulgarians, Wallachians, and Ottomans. Today it is a major port and center of tourism, beaches and archeology the main draw.

www.romaniatourism.com/constanta.html

Eol777, Str. Aviator Vasile Craiu nr 3, Jud Constanta, Romania; *www.hosteleol777.ro*, T:0727555556, *razvan_jianu@yahoo.com;* $13bed, Kitchen:Y, B'fast:N, WiFi:Y, Pvt. room:Y, Locker:N, Recep:ltd;
Note: luggage room, laundry, parking, free airport pickup!

SIBIU is a Transylvanian fortified city and historically the most important of the seven Saxon cities of the region. Ottomans and Austro-Hungarians came and went, and after WWI the region became part of Romania. Many Germans left after WWII and the advent of Communism, but not all. One became mayor. The historical center is the main attraction for tourism. There are three squares and remains of the city walls, the Brukenthal Museum, a massive Lutheran cathedral, an Orthodox cathedral, and an 18th-century Roman Catholic Church.

www.romaniatourism.com/sibiu.html

Felinarul Hostel, Strada Felinarului, Sibiu, Romania; *www.felinarulhostelsibiu.ro*, T:0269235260, *info@felinarulhostelsibiu.ro;* $16bed, Kitchen:Y, B'fast:Y, WiFi:Y, Pvt.room:N, Locker:Y, Recep:ltd;
Note: café-bar, parking, luggage rm, laundry, tour desk, bike rent, central

Sibiu Travelers Hostel/Villa Treilor, St. Teilor, Sibiu, Romania; *www.sibiutravelershostel.com*, T:0765816544, *info@villateilor.com;* $16bed, Kitchen:Y, B'fast:Y, WiFi:Y, Pvt. room:N, Locker:Y, Recep:24/7;

Note: luggage room, laundry, parking, forex, c.c. ok, near train/bus

Old Town Hostel, Piaţa Mică 26, Sibiu, Romania; *www.hostelsibiu.ro/*, T:0269216445, *contact@hostelsibiu.ro*; $15bed, Kitchen:Y, B'fast:N, WiFi:Y, Pvt. room:Y, Locker:N, Recep:24/7;
Note: central, luggage room, laundry, tour desk, "nice old building"

Flying Time Hostel, Strada Gheorghe Lazăr 6, Sibiu, Romania; *www.sibiuhostel.ro/en/*, T:0369730179, *booking@sibiuhostel.ro*; $13bed, Kitchen:Y, B'fast:N, WiFi:Y, Pvt. room:Y, Locker:Y, Recep:24/7;
Note: bar/café, laundry, luggage room, TV, central

SIGHISOARA is another Saxon town in Transylvania and is an exemplary medieval town. The town surrounds a hill, on top of which stands a citadel with a ring of walls, nine standing towers, and a number of medieval churches. It was a center of arts and crafts and associated trades. It was also the home of Vlad Dracul, Vlad the Impaler's father. Ouch!

www.romaniatourism.com/sighisoara.html

Nathan's Villa, Strada Libertăţii, Sighisoara, Romania; *sighisora.nathansvilla.com*, T:0265772546, *sighisora@nathansvilla.com*; $15bed, Kitchen:Y, B'fast:Y, WiFi:Y, Pvt. room:N, Locker:Y, Recep:ltd;
Note: luggage ok, laundry, parking, tour desk, rooms in basement, central

Burg Hostel, Strada Bastionului, Sighisoara, Romania; *www.burghostel.ro*, T:0265778489, *burghostel@ibz.ro*; $12bed, Kitchen:N, B'fast:$, WiFi:Y, Pvt. room:Y, Locker:N, Recep:24/7;
Note: resto/bar, tour desk, luggage room, TV, central

Gia Hostel, Str. Libertatii 41. Romania, jud Mures; *www.hotelgia.ro*, T:+40265772486, *office@cazareinsighisoara.ro*; $11bed, Kitchen:Y, B'fast:N, WiFi:Y, Pvt. room:Y, Locker:N, Recep:24/7;
Note: laundry, tour desk, parking, near train, old hotel turned hostel

SUCEAVA is located in the far north of the country, near the border with Ukraine. It is the former capital of Moldavia, and from 1775 until 1918 it was part of the Austrian Habsburg Empire, after which it was incorporated into Romania. It was heavily industrialized during the Communist Era, but since then has developed some tourism. There are numerous historical churches, museums, and an historical citadel, including the 14th-century Mirăuţi Church, the 16th-century Church of St. George, and the Church of St. Demetrius.

www.romaniatourism.com/suceava.html

Irene's Hostel, Strada Armenească 4, Suceava, Romania;
www.ireneshostel.ro/, T:0744292588, *ireneshostel@gmail.com;* $15bed,
Kitchen:Y, B'fast:N, WiFi:Y, Pvt. room:Y, Locker:N, Recep:24/7;
Note: laundry, tour desk, prkng, luggage ok, @ bus terminal, central

Lary Hostel, Str. Vlaicu Aurel, 195, Suceava, Romania;
www.hostelsuceava.ro, T:0747086329, *laryhostel@yahoo.com*, $15bed,
Kitchen:N, B'fast:$, WiFi:Y, Pvt. room:Y, Locker:Y, Recep:24/7;
Note: bar/club, parking, laundry, c.c. ok, tour desk, not central

TIMISOARA is Romania's third largest city, and is located in the western region of Banat, only a stone's throw from Serbia. It is documented from the thirteenth century as a part of Hungary. In 1552 it was conquered by the Ottoman Turks and became capital of a new province created by them. That was the status until 1716 when it came under Austrian rule. As a part of Europe it became industrialized and modernized, opening the region's first beer factory in 1717, and becoming the first city in Europe with electric lights, in fact. After WWI it became part of Romania, Communist until the 1989 revolution. Landmarks include the Roman Catholic cathedral, the Serbian cathedral, and the regional museum, housed in a restored 14th C. palace. Its main tourist attraction is its lack of tourist attractions.

www.timisoara.com/

Hostel Costel, Str. Petru Sfetca Nr.1 (ex-Vidra), Timisoara, Romania; *www.hostel-costel.ro/*, T:0726240223, *office@hostel-costel.ro/gallery*, $12bed, Kitchen:Y, B'fast:N, WiFi:Y, Pvt. room:Y, Locker:Y, Recep:24/7;
Note: bike rent, parking, luggage room, laundry, TV, pets ok

Freeborn Hostel, Strada Patriarh Miron Cristea 3, Timisoara, Romania; *www.freebornhostel.com/*, T:0743438534, *f reebornhostel@gmail.com;*
$12bed, Kitchen:Y, B'fast:N, WiFi:Y, Pvt. room:Y, Locker:Y, Recep:24/7;
Note: wheelchair ok, parking, tour desk, forex, TV, luggage ok, laundry

21) Russia

The legacy of the USSR casts a long shadow over the image of Russia, but that's an image that will fade in proportion to the distance from that era. More than anything else Russia is huge, occupying more than ten percent of the planet's available land after the world's most massive migration ever, that of Russians east to Siberia and the Pacific. This all finally coalesced into a state so recently that it's fairly well documented, starting with the proto-Viking Varangian "Rus" (get it?) around Kiev in the ninth century AD and re-constituted in the Grand Duchy of Moscow's post-Mongol Era, when it fancied itself the "Third Rome" picking up the pieces after the fall of Constantinople. Then followed the Enlightenment, Peter the Great's entry into Europe, and finally the 20th century, with its WWII decimation and its Communism. With the final demise of the USSR and a decade of ineffective leaders, local mafia, and decline, Russia is finally regaining its balance and status in the world (thanks at least in part to high oil prices).

Unfortunately tourism doesn't seem to have changed much since the early days when commie paranoia was matched only by the desperate need for hard currency. Currently they could not care less. Nobody will be waiting at baggage claim to buy your used Levis, and Russian women will not follow you down the street wanting to get into your used Levis. Yet there is still a level of unnecessary formalities and bureaucracy almost unknown elsewhere. That means a super-expensive visa, which means a Letter of Invitation, basically just a meaningless extra formality and charge. Then once you get there, you're supposed to register everywhere you go, which carries with it another charge. Supposedly they check, but never really do, still you never know. All this ups the price of an already expensive country. Now Moscow is certainly unique, and so is Saint Petersburg, but besides that, I'm not sure what the big attraction is, except the trans-Siberian train, of course. Russian is the language; *ruble* is currency; phone code is +7.

www.russia-travel.com/

IRKUTSK is the main city of the Siberian oblast (province) of the same name and a major stop on the trans-Siberian railroad near Lake Baikal. Originally a fur and gold trading center out east, by the 19th century Irkutsk was already receiving political deportees, many of them Decembrists (no, not the rock band), part of the revolt against Czar Nicholas I. The town also saw fierce battles during the Revolution, but now is a center of education, culture, and the aircraft industry. The reservoir is a World Heritage site. The city has many wooden houses on tree-lined streets.

www.waytorussia.net/Siberia/Irkutsk/Guide.html

Baikaler Hostel, Lenin Street Building 9 Apt 11, Irkutsk, Russia; *www.baikaler.com/*, T:8(3952)336240, *info@baikaler.com*; $20bed, Kitchen:Y, B'fast:N, WiFi:Y, Pvt. room:N, Locker:N, Recep:ltd;
Note: tours, also eco-hostel in Listvyanka, overbook go elsewhere

Admiral Hostel, Cheremhovsky pereulok, Bldg 6, Apt1 Irkutsk; *www.irkutskhostel.irk.ru*, T:8(3952)742440, *baikalhostel@irk.ru*; $20bed, Kitchen:Y, B'fast:N, WiFi:Y, Pvt. room:Y, Locker:N, Recep:ltd;
Note: laundry, luggage room, TV, coffee & tea, hard to find, central

Trans-Sib Hostel, Sportivniy Street, Bldg 9 Ap 8, Irkutsk, Russia; *www.irkutsk-hostel.com/*, T:+79041180652, *transsib-hostel@mail.ru;* $17bed, Kitchen:Y, B'fast:Y, WiFi:Y, Pvt. room:Y, Locker:N, Recep:24/7;
Note: tour desk, luggage room, laundry, forex, near train, walk to town

Baikal Hostel, Lermontov Str. 136, apt. 1, Irkutsk, Russia; *www.baikalhostels.ru*, T:+73952940798, *booking@baikalhostels.ru*; $19bed, Kitchen:Y, B'fast:Y, WiFi:Y, Pvt. room:Y, Locker:N, Recep:24/7;
Note: tour desk, laundry, luggage room, bit far & hard to find

KALININGRAD was a German city known as Konigsberg, going way back to the Knights Templar, Prussia and then Germany before the USSR decided to snatch it as the spoils of WWII. The German inhabitants were all evicted and forced to settle elsewhere. The *oblast* of the same name is an enclave even smaller in size than the Baltic countries, NATO nations which now separate it from not-so-motherly Russia. The city is a confusing conglomerate of modern Russian buildings and old German ones.

russiatrek.org/kaliningrad-city

Amigos Hostel, Epronovskaya st. 20-102, Kaliningrad, Russia; *amigoshostel.ru*, T:8(911)4852157, *kld.hostels@hotmail.com*; $19bed, Kitchen:Y, B'fast:N, WiFi:Y, Pvt. room:N, Locker:Y, Recep:24/7; Note: 13th floor, lift, luggage room, lift, bar, central

MOSCOW is the heart of the beast, of course, documented from at least the mid-12th century and prominent since the 1300's as the Grand Duchy of Moscow. Before that it was just a village on the river Moskva. It lost some prominence in the 1700's with the founding of Saint Petersburg, but regained it in the Soviet era. It withstood the onslaught and sieges of Napoleon in the early 1800's, ditto Hitler in WWII, so naturally became a little bit defensive about the challenge laid down by the US during the Cold War. Already the head of a 15-nation USSR with a strong buffer zone in Europe's own Warsaw Pact, Moscow increasingly found itself at the center of an empire spreading (ideologically at least) all over the world, first China and Mongolia then North Korea, Cuba, Vietnam, Laos, Cambodia, with more to come, increasingly more totalitarian disctatorships than economic socialists—Angola, Ethiopia, Libya, Syria, Nicaragua, Afghanistan (sound of needle scratching long and hard over vinyl)—and the rest is history.

Communism fell, and after a rough start, Moscow's future is bright at the head of a reinvigorated Russia, as long as the Mafia gets their cut. It's more than a little bit ironic that twenty years after communism's fall, Moscow has more billionaires than any other place in the world, and I doubt that the GINI poverty index is so good, either. Moscow's Commie rep as a drab collection of khaki-colored comrades sipping cold soup in cement-grey cell-blocks is a thing of the distant past. Today Moscow puts the 'vibe' in 'vibrant' with the word 'nonstop' plastered all over, from café to pub to all-night disco. And of course they've always had some of the finest literature, music, dance, and art the world has ever seen.

Catch the classic rock band Mumiy Troll. And there's still the Kremlin and St. Basil's and Matrioshka dolls just waiting to have their outer layers removed.

The Kremlin includes the Saviour (Spasskaya) Tower, leading to Red Square. Also on the Red Square is the St. Nicholas (Nikolskaya) Tower. The two other principal gate towers—the Trinity (Troitskaya) Tower, with a bridge and outer barbican (the Kutafya Tower), and the Borovitskaya Tower—rise from the western wall. Churches and other landmarks include the Cathedral of the Assumption, the Cathedral of the Annunciation, the Palace of Facets, the Armoury Palace and Armoury Museum. Hostels are good but not cheap, and then there are the regulatory hassles. Persevere. It's got to be worth it for that train, right?

www.moscow-life.com/

Green ManGO Hostel, Novaya Basmannaya St 25/2, Moscow, Russia; *www.greenmangohostel.com*, 4992611076, *info@greenmangohostel.com;* $26bed, Kitchen:Y, B'fast:N, WiFi:Y, Pvt. room:N, Locker:N, Recep:24/7;
Note: bike rent, lift, laundry, a/c, c.c., TV, hard to find, modern, central

Godzillas Hostel, Bolshoi Karetnyy 6, Apt 5 (1st Floor), Moscow, Russia; *www.godzillashostel.com/*, T:+7(495)6994223; *info@godzillashostel.com;* $28bed, Kitchen:Y, B'fast:N, WiFi:Y, Pvt. room:Y, Locker:N, Recep:24/7;
Note: luggage room, laundry, tour desk, ATM, Sat TV, no alcohol

Chocolate Hostel, Degtyarny per. 15, Bldg 1, Apt.4, I-com 004, Moscow; *www.chocohostel.com/*, T:+7(495)9712046, *contacts@chocohostel.com;*
$24bed, Kitchen:Y, B'fast:Y, WiFi:Y, Pvt. room:Y, Locker:Y, Recep:24/7;
Note: luggage ok, laundry, tour desk, c.c. ok, central, hard to find, bliny!

Moscow Home Hostel, 2 Neopalimovsky Per. 1/12, (1st Fl), Moscow; *www.moshostel.com/*, T:+7(495)7782445, *info@moshostel.com*; $15bed, Kitchen:Y, B'fast:N, WiFi:Y, Pvt. room:Y, Locker:N, Recep:24/7;

Note: luggage ok, laundry, parking, tour desk, c.c. ok, central

HM Hostel Moscow, #14, 4th Fl, M. Afanasyevskiy per 1/33, m. Arbat; *www.hostel-moscow.com/*, T+7(495)7788501, *info@hostel-moscow.com;* $24bed, Kitchen:Y, B'fast:$, WiFi:Y, Pvt. room:N, Locker:N, Recep:24/7;
Note: bar, tour desk luggage ok, laundry, a/c, forex, central

TNT Hostel, 5 Zvonarskiy pereulok, 3rd Fl #6, Moscow, Russia; *www.tnthostel.com/*, T:8(495)9730501, *info@tnthostel.com;*$17bed, Kitchen:Y, B'fast:N, WiFi:Y, Pvt. room:Y, Locker:N, Recep:24/7;
Note: laundry, parking c.c. ok, LOI, no signs outside, clubs & pubs

Moscow Style Hostel, Tverskaya St. 15 App.80, Moscow; *www.mos-style.com* T:8(926)4936225; $24bed, Kitchen:Y, B'fast:Y, WiFi:Y, Pvt. room:Y, Locker:Y, Recep:24/7;
Note: luggage ok, laundry, tour desk, a/c, central, homestay

Comrade Hostel, Maroseyka Street, 11, 3rd Fl, Moscow, Russia; *comradehostel.com/*, T:+74997098760 *info@comradehostel.com*; $22bed, Kitchen:Y, B'fast:N, WiFi:Y, Pvt. room:Y, Locker:N, Recep:24/7;
Note: LOI, forex, luggage ok, laundry, prkng, no lift, central, coffee

Trans-Siberian Hostel, Barashevskiy Pereulok 12, Moscow, Russia; *www.tshostel.com/*, T:+74959162030, *info@tshostel.com;* $20bed, Kitchen:N, B'fast:Y, WiFi:Y, Pvt. room:Y, Locker:Y, Recep:24/7;
Note: tour desk, luggage ok, laundry, prkng, a/c, LOI, central, mkt near

Napoleon Hostel, Maly Zlatoustinskiy St, Dom 2, 4th Fl, Moscow; *www.napoleonhostel.com/*, T:8(495)6245978, *info@napoleonhostel.com;* $20bed, Kitchen:Y, B'fast:N, WiFi:Y, Pvt. room:N, Locker:Y, Recep:24/7;
Note: LOI, resto/bar, tour desk, prkng, a/c, c.c. ok, 4th Fl no lift, central

A la Russe Hotel & Hostel, 5, Voznesenskiy St, Moscow, Russia; *www.hotelalaruss.com/*, T:8(495)6970503, *info@hotelalaruss.com;*

$15bed, Kitchen:Y, B'fast:$, WiFi:Y, Pvt. room:Y, Locker:Y, Recep:24/7;
Note: wheelchair ok, parking, tour desk, c.c. ok, long-timers, central

Suharevka Hostel, Bolshaya Suharevskaya Sq, 16/18 apt. 5, Moscow; *www.suharevkahotel.ru/*, T:89104203446(RU), *info@suharevkahotel.ru;* $25bed, Kitchen:Y, B'fast:N, WiFi:Y, Pvt. room:Y, Locker:Y, Recep:24/7;
Note: LOI, tour desk, luggage room, c.c. ok

Da! Hostel, (Old) Arbat, 11, Moscow, Russia; *da-hostel.com/*, T:+7(495)6915577, *info@da-hostel.ru;* $19bed, Kitchen:Y, B'fast:N, WiFi:Y, Pvt. room:Y, Locker:Y, Recep:24/7,
Note: arpt trans, lift, luggage rm, laundry, tour desk, central, no lift

Apple Hostel, Big Spasoglinitshevsky Lane 6/1, Moscow, Russia; *www.applehostel.ru*, T:+7(916)3355333, *applehostel@mail.ru;* $21bed, Kitchen:Y, B'fast:N, WiFi:Y, Pvt. room:N, Locker:Y, Recep:24/7;
Note: bike, lift, luggage rm, laundry, tour desk, parking, Kitai-G metro

iVAN Hostel, Petrovsky pereulok, 1/30, apt. 23., Moscow; *ivanhostel.com*/, T:+79164071178, *ivanhostel@gmail.com*; $26bed, Kitchen:Y, B'fast:N, WiFi:Y, Pvt. room:Y, Locker:Y, Recep:24/7;
Note: arpt trans, lift, luggage room, laundry, parking, central, basic

Bear/Arbatskaya, Bolshaya Molchanovka 23, fl#5, *bh3@bear-hostels.ru;*
Bear Hostels/Mayakovskaya, Sadovaya-Kudrinskaya 32, Bldg.2, fl#4; *www.bear-hostels.com*, T:+7(495)5404361, *bh2@bear-hostels.ru*; $17bed, Kitchen:Y, B'fast:N, Wi-Fi:Y, Pvt. room:Y, Locker:Y, Recep:24/7;
Note: bikes, lift, luggage room, laundry, parking, tour desk

Taganka Hostel, Marksistskaia St 34/2, Vorontsovskaya St 35B-2; *en.tagankahostel.ru*/, T:(495)9116969, *info@tagankahostel.ru;* $20bed, Kitchen:Y, B'fast:$, Wi-Fi:Y, Pvt. room:N, Locker:Y, Recep:24/7;
Note: café/bar, tour desk, pool, luggage room, parking

Capital Hostel, 5/6, Malaya Ordynka, Moscow, Russia; *capitalhostel.com/*,T:+74959591347, *info@capitalhostel.com*; $26bed, Kitchen:N, B'fast:N, Wi-Fi:Y, Pvt. room:Y, Locker:N, Recep:24/7; Note: arpt trans, lift, parking, luggage room, central, cozy

ST. PETERSBURG is Russia's second city of course, both in population and importance. It is also one of the newest, purpose-built by Peter the Great (note the similarity in names) to serve as his western-looking imperial capital, a function it served except for four short years until 1917. So Peter captured the land from Sweden in 1704, and by 1712 it was serving as capital, though the treaty that ended the war wasn't in effect until 1721. Cool, huh? Just take what you want, as long as you size up your competitor's, uh... army, first. Russia also moved the capital of Finland to Helsinki, just so the two capitals could be closer, any symbolism your own. With WWI and Bolshevism in full swing, SPb was first renamed Petrograd (to not sound so German), then "Red" Petrograd (to sound more Commie), then finally Leningrad (to honor the architect of the matrix... er, I mean 'revolution').

St. Petersburg finally returned to its original name after "falling" to capitalism in 1991. Today it's still a great seaport and Russia's most Western city. Tourist sights include Palace square, the canals, and my favorite, the Hermitage Museum. Others are Decembrists' (or Dekabristovs') Square, the buildings of the former Senate and Synod, the Horse Guards Riding School, St. Isaac's Square and cathedral of the same name. The main thoroughfare Nevsky Prospekt contains the Stroganov, Shuvalov, and Anichkov palaces and several churches, of which the most notable are St. Peter's Lutheran Church, St. Catherine's Roman Catholic Church, and the Kazan Cathedral. Hostels tend to want cash and the quality varies wildly. If you need a LOI, then that's a consideration, since some do it, some don't, and charges vary. St. Pete is the beer capital of Russia (burp).

petersburgcity.com/

Apple Hostel Italy, Italyanskaya St. 12, 2nd Fl, St Petersburg, Russia; *www.applehostel.ru*, T:8(812)4588830, *applehostel@mail.ru;* $15bed, Kitchen:Y, B'fast:N, WiFi:Y, Pvt. room:Y, Locker:Y, Recep:24/7; Note: prkng, tour desk, laundry, luggage ok, cozy, hard to find

Soul Kitchen Hostel, 1st Sovietskaya 12, app 1, St Petersburg; *soulkitchenhostel.com/*, $19bed, *soulkitchenhostel@gmail.com;* Kitchen:Y, B'fast:Y, WiFi:Y, Pvt. room:Y, Locker:Y, Recep:24/7; Note: age limit 44, cash only, tour desk, luggage ok, laundry

MIR Hostel, Nevsky Ave, 16, St. Petersburg, Russia; *mirhostel.com/*, T:8(812)5710641, *mirhostel@gmail.com;* $15bed, Kitchen:N, B'fast:Y, WiFi:Y, Pvt. room:Y, Locker:Y, Recep:24/7; Note: cash, LOI, free tour, free dinks, laundry, luggage ok, no lift

Hostel Pilau, Rubinshteyna Street 38, 1st Fl Apt 12, St. Petersburg; *www.hostelpilau.com/*, T:+78125721075, *director@hostelpilau.com;* $18bed, Kitchen:Y, B'fast:N, WiFi:Y, Pvt. room:N, Locker:N, Recep:24/7;
Note: prkng, tour desk, c.c. ok, coffee/tea, near bus/train

Acme Hostel, 11, Sadovaya Str, Saint Petersburg, Russia; *www.acme-hotel.com*, T:+7(812)3371223, *info@acme-hotel.com;* $14bed, Kitchen:Y, B'fast:N, WiFi:Y, Pvt. room:Y, Locker:N, Recep:24/7; Note: 4th Fl no lift, tour desk, luggage room, laundry, central

Griboideva Hostel, Kaznacheiskaya 6/13, St Petersburg, Russia; *www.griboedova71.ru/*, T:(812)3156948, *reservations@griboedova71.ru;* $14bed, Kitchen:Y, B'fast:N, WiFi:Y, Pvt. room:N, Locker:Y, Recep:24/7; Note: parking, laundry, luggage room, TV, c.c. ok, central

NevskyHostel, Bol'shaya Konyushennaya ulitsa, St Petersburg, Russia; *www.nevskyhostels.com/*, T:+7(812)3121206, *booking@hon.ru;* $15bed, Kitchen:Y, B'fast:$, WiFi:Y, Pvt. room:Y, Locker:Y, Recep:24/7; Note: luggage room, laundry, tour desk, c.c. ok

St Petersburg - Location Hostel, 8 Admiralteisky Ave, St. Petersburg; *www.hihostels.com*. T:+7(812)4906429, *info@location-hostel.ru*; $20bed, Kitchen:Y, B'fast:N, WiFi:Y, Pvt. room:Y, Locker:Y, Recep:24/Note: coffee & tea, laundry, luggage room, central

Na Muchnom, 25, Sadovaya str., St Petersburg, Russia;

en.namuchnom.ru/, T:+7(812)3100412; $24bed, Kitchen:N, B'fast:Y, WiFi:N, Pvt. room:Y, Locker:Y, Recep:24/7;
Note: tour desk, c.c. ok, central

Cuba Hostel, Kazanskaya ulitsa, 5, Saint Petersburg, Russia; *www.cubahostel.ru/*, T:8(812)9217115, *cubahostel@gmail.com*; $16bed, Kitchen:Y, B'fast:N, WiFi:Y, Pvt. room:N, Locker:Y, Recep:24/7;
Note: bar, parking, tour desk, laundry, luggage room, good location

St. Petersburg Intl. Hostel, 28 3rd Sovetskaya St, St. Petersburg; *www.ryh.ru/*, T:+7(812)3298018, *ryh@ryh.ru;* $24bed, Kitchen:Y, B'fast:N, WiFi:Y, Pvt. room:N, Locker:N, Recep:24/7;
Note: tour desk, luggage room, laundry, a/c, c.c. ok

Puppet Hostel, 12 Ulitsa Nekrasova, St Petersburg, Russia; *www.hostel-puppet.ru*, T:+7(812)2725401, *info@hostel-puppet.ru;* $24bed, Kitchen:Y, B'fast:$, WiFi:Y, Pvt. room:Y, Locker:N, Recep:24/7;
Note: tour desk, luggage room, free visa reg., lift

Sabrina Hotel, Voznesenskiy pros. 41, St Petersburg, Russia; *www.sabrina-hotel.ru/*, T:+7(812)3147200, *reception@sabrina-hotel.ru;* $13bed, Kitchen:N, B'fast:Y, WiFi:Y, Pvt. room:Y, Locker:N, Recep:24/7;
Note: parking, tour desk, laundry, luggage room, a/c, c.c. ok

Hostel Metro Tour, 47, Blagodatnaya str, St Petersburg, Russia; *www.hostelmetro.com/*, T:+7(812)3696451, *admin@hostelmetro.spb.ru*; $11bed, Kitchen:Y, B'fast:N, WiFi:Y, Pvt. room:Y, Locker:N, Recep:24/7;
Note: tour desk, laundry, luggage room, c.c. ok

SOCHI is Russia's largest resort with the dubious distinction of being some 90mi/145km long, spead along the Black Sea coast and near the Caucasus Mountains. Being part of the Caucasus region the town is confusingly diverse, having changed hands and religions frequently. Long known as a subtropical resort for Russians, today it is best known as the site of the 2014 Winter Olympics.

www.russia-ukraine-travel.com/sochi.html

Mountain Skit Hostel, Achishhovskaya str. 8, Sochi, Russia; *www.skithostel.ru/*, **T:+7(964)9400470,** *skithostel@mail.ru;* $10bed, Kitchen:Y, B'fast:$, WiFi:Y, Pvt. room:Y, Locker:Y, Recep:24/7; Note: luggage ok, laundry, tour desk, prkng, homestay, hard to find

ULAN ADE is one of the largest cities of eastern Siberia and capital of Buryatia. Buryat Mongols were the original inhabitants and even today make up over 20% of the population. As such it is also a center for Tibetan Buddhism, the religion of Mongolia. It is located on the Trans-Siberian railway at the head of the branch line to Ulan Bator, and is a major regional trade center between Russia, China, and Mongolia. There is an ethnographic museum and a sculpted head of Lenin that weighs forty-two tons. Ulan Ade was closed to foreigners until 1991.

www.waytorussia.net/Siberia/UlanUde/UlanUde.html

Ulan Ade Traveler's House, 18 App, 63 Bldg, Lenin St, Ulan Ude; *uuhostel.com/hostel/*, T:+79503916325, *uuhostel@gmail.com*; $22bed, Kitchen:N, B'fast:Y, WiFi:Y, Pvt. room:N, Locker:N, Recep:24/7; Note: tour desk, forex, laundry, luggage room

YEKATERINBURG was founded in 1723 and is the fourth-largest city in Russia (bet you didn't know that, did you?) and sits more-or-less smack on the line geographically separating Europe from Asia, the Ural mountain range. It's also where the last czar was killed. It's also where Gary Powers was shot down in his US spy plane. More importantly, it's a stop on the Trans-Siberian line, a good place to break the trip between Moscow, Irkutsk and/or Ulan-Ade. Boris Yeltsin spent much of his career here.

www.ekaterinburg.com/

Europe Asia Yekaterinburg, Tchaikovskogo 75/216, Yekaterinburg; *eayh.ucoz.ru/*, T:+7(343)2192788, *interchange70@narod.ru;* $19bed, Kitchen:Y, B'fast:N, WiFi:Y, Pvt. room:N, Locker:Y, Recep:24/7;

Note: cash, luggage ok, laundry, forex, tour desk, prkng, a/c, hard find

Domino Hotel, Apt. 149 60 Chelyuskintsev St, Yekaterinburg, Russia; *dominohotel.ru/*, T:+79221815460; $27bed, Kitchen:Y, B'fast:N, WiFi:Y, Pvt. room:N, Locker:Y, Recep:24/7
Note: homestay, arpt trans, parking, laundry, luggage room, hard find

22) Serbia

Of the three Serbo-Croatian-Bosnian-speaking countries, Serbia is the most Eastern of the group, with Cyrillic alphabet and Orthodox religion and a close political ally in Russia. It used to be a Roman colony (Emperor Constantine was born here) and then was ruled by the Byzantine Empire, its own empire, then the Ottoman, before asserting its independence again in the late 1800's. It scored major territorial gains against Bulgaria. It even started WWI, and won.

Thus emboldened Serbia continued its rise by forming the Kingdom of Serbs, Croats, and Slovenes (later to become Yugoslavia) with the other Balkan states, of which it was the most prominent and longest-lasting member. After decimation in WWII, communist "partisans" rose to power in the aftermath and ruled without opposition until 1989 when Slobodan Milosevic's rise to power and attempts to limit regional autonomy induced the breakup of the federation and the start of war. Crimes against humanity ensued, and Serbia has been an international pariah until recently. *Dinar* (RSD) is the currency; Serbian (Coatian, Bosnian) is the language; the calling code is +381.

www.guides-serbia.com/

BELGRADE is the capital and largest city of Serbia, located at the confluence of the Danube and Sava rivers. This is a good example of a city belonging to a place, not a people. It was successively Thraco-Dacian, Celt, Roman, Slav, Bulgarian, Ottoman, and Habsburg, before becoming the capital of Serbia again in 1841. It was the capital of Yugoslavia from inception to dissolution 1918-2006. All of which says nothing about Constantine the Great or Attila the Hun or Frederick Barbarossa or Suleyman the Magnificent or Prince Maximilian, but they were all here. It was at the heart of WWI, and emerged stronger in the aftermath. It tried to remain neutral in WWII, but didn't succeed. The Axis Powers invaded and occupied, until liberated by Tito's partisans. Though communist, Belgrade was prominent in the nonaligned movement. Yugoslavia's breakup and Serbia's unwillingness to allow it finally hit home when NATO bombed Belgrade in the Kosovo War in 1999. Mass demonstrations removed Slobodan Milosevic from office the next year.

By virtue of its size, Belgrade is the center of almost everything in Serbia: industry, fashion, media, etc. It took some hits from NATO bombing in the Kosovo war, but it wasn't really known for its architecture anyway. What it IS known for is nightlife. Hostel quality is generally good and there is some diversity and creativity, too, like free beer. Unfortunately there is also a lot of smoking inside, and kitchens are not a given. There are a LOT of them, too, maybe the most in the world, which seems a bit disproportionate, so percentage-wise, they're a bit under-represented here. This may be the one place in the world where you could just show up in town, start walking, and find a hostel. Have fun. Despite all the rape, pillage, and ethnic cleansing, Serbians really can be very nice people. Give 'em a chance.

www.tob.rs/en/index.php

Montmartre Hostel Belgrade, Nušićeva 17/5, Belgrade, Serbia; *montmartre-hostel.com/*, T:0113224157, *montmartrehostel@gmail.com;* $17bed, Kitchen:Y, B'fast:Y, WiFi:Y, Pvt. room:Y, Locker:Y, Recep:24/7;
Note: welcome drink, luggage room, laundry, a/c, good location

Hedonist Hostel, Simina 7, Belgrade; *hedonisthostelbelgrade.com,* T:0113284798, *office@hedonisthostelbelgrade.com*; $17bed, Kitchen:Y, B'fast:N, WiFi:Y, Pvt. room:N, Locker:Y, Recep:8a>11p;
Note: luggage room, laundry, travel desk, a/c

Time Hostel, Cara Lazara St, #9, Apt #3, Belgrade, Serbia; *time-hostels.com/*, T:+381(0)113285160; $20bed, Kitchen:Y, B'fast:N, WiFi:Y, Pvt. room:Y, Locker:Y, Recep:24/7;
Note: laundry, luggage ok, parking, tour desk, central, supermkt

Chillton 2, Vase Carapica (Vasina) 15, Belgrade, Serbia;
www.chilltonhostel.com/, T:0113283333, *chillton2@gmail.com*; $20bed, Kitchen:N, B'fast:Y, WiFi:Y, Pvt. room:Y, Locker:Y, Recep:24/7;
Note: 2N min. stay, luggage room, laundry, free tour, a/c

Manga Hostel, Resavska 7, Belgrade, Serbia;
www.mangahostel.com/, T:+381113243877, *fun@mangahostel.com*; $17bed, Kitchen:Y, B'fast:N, WiFi:Y, Pvt. room:Y, Locker:Y, Recep:24/7;
Note: luggage room, laundry, a/c, tricky to find, coffee & tea

Spirit Hostel, Brace Baruh 20b, Belgrade, Serbia;
www.spirithostel.com/, T:+381112920055, *office@spirithostel.com*; $20bed, Kitchen:Y, B'fast:Y, WiFi:Y, Pvt.room:Y, Locker:Y, Recep:>12m;
Note: luggage room, laundry, coffee & tea, welcome drink

BB's House, Bulevar despota Stefana 63, Belgrade, Serbia;
www.bbshouse.rs/, T:062623730, *bbshouse63@gmail.com*; $18bed, Kitchen:Y, B'fast:Y, WiFi:Y, Pvt. room:Y, Locker:Y, Recep:24/7;
Note: luggage room, laundry, tour desk, c.c. ok, good location

Backpacker's Lounge, Cika Ljubina 10, Main Republic Sq, Belgrade;
www.hostelbelgrade.net/, T:0112627483, *backpackerslounge@gmail.com;* $13bed, Kitchen:Y, B'fast:N, WiFi:Y, Pvt. room:N, Locker:Y, Recep:24/7;
Note: luggage ok, laundry, tour desk, wheelchair ok, a/c, 4th Fl, parties

1001 Nights Hostel, Bulevar Kralja Aleksandra 40, Belgrade, Serbia;
www.1001nightshostel.com/, 0113247658, *1001nightshostel@gmail.com;* $15bed, Kitchen:N, B'fast:N, WiFi:Y, Pvt. room:Y, Locker:Y, Recep:24/7;
Note: welcome drink, coffee tea, luggage ok, prkng, free tour, central

Hostel 360, 21 Knez Mihailova St, Belgrade, Serbia;
hostel360.com/, T:+381112634957, *skile@sbb.rs*; $20bed, Kitchen:Y, B'fast:N, WiFi:Y, Pvt. room:Y, Locker:Y, Recep:24/7;

Note: luggage room, laundry, lift, a/c, c.c. ok, 5th Fl. bad lift, center

Hostel Zetska, Zetska 5, Belgrade, Serbia;
www.hostelzetska5.rs, T:+381621648892, *info@hostelzetska5.rs;* $17bed, Kitchen:N, B'fast:N, WiFi:Y, Pvt. room:Y, Locker:Y, Desk hr:24/7;
Note: luggage room, tour desk, laundry, a/c, central

Hostel Kris, Kneza Milosa 54, Belgrade, Serbia;
hostelkris.weebly.com/, T:+381665010206, *hostelkris@yahoo.com;*
$13bed, Kitchen:Y, B'fast:N, WiFi:Y, Pvt. room:N, Locker:N, Recep:ltd;
Note: cozy, laundry, luggage room, parking, a/c

Star Hostel, Cara Urosa 37, Belgrade, Serbia;
www.starhostelbelgrade.com/, T:0112184104, *hostel_star@yahoo.com;*
$17bed, Kitchen:Y, B'fast:Y, WiFi:Y, Pvt. room:Y, Locker:Y, Recep:24/7;
Note: coffee & tea, bar, tour desk, luggage room, central

Sun Hostel, Novopazarska 25, Belgrade, Serbia;
www.sun.hostel.com/, T:(0)641201065, *hostel.sun@gmail.com;* $9bed, Kitchen:Y, B'fast:N, WiFi:Y, Pvt. room:Y, Locker:Y, Recep:24/7;
Note: party atmosphere, little far to center, laundry, tour desk, forex, a/c

Arka Barka Floating Hostel, Bulevar Nikole Tesle bb, Park Usce;
www.arkabarka.net/, T:0649253507, *arkabarkahostel@gmail.com;*
$20bed, Kitchen:N, B'fast:Y, WiFi:Y, Pvt. room:Y, Locker:Y, Recep:24/7;
Note: bar, luggage room, parking, on river not central

Good Morning Hostel, Takovska 36-38, Belgrade, Serbia;
goodmorninghostels.com/, T:0113295031, *info@goodmorninghostels.com;*
$10bed, Kitchen:N, B'fast:N, WiFi:Y, Pvt. room:Y, Locker:Y, Recep:ltd;
Note: luggage room fee, laundry, tour desk, parking, a/c

Green Studio Hostel, Karađorđeva 69, Apt 42, Belgrade, Serbia;
greenstudiohostel.com/, T:0637562357, *greenstudiohostel@gmail.com;*

$19bed, Kitchen:Y, B'fast:N, WiFi:Y, Pvt. room:Y, Locker:Y, Recep:24/7;
Note: bar, prkng, forex, tour desk, luggage ok, laundry, by train, coffee/tea

Go2 Hostel, Prizrenska 1, Belgrade, Serbia;
go2hostelbelgrade.com/, T:0648294324, *office@go2hostelbelgrade.com;*
$10bed, Kitchen:N, B'fast:$, WiFi:Y, Pvt.room:Y, Locker:Y, Recep:24/7;
Note: near supermkt, central, tour desk, luggage ok, laundry, a/c, c.c. ok

Belgrade Center Hostel, Zeleni Venac 4, *belgrade.centre@gmail.com;*
T:0638718028, *belgradecentrehostel.blogspot.com/*; $11bed,
Kitchen:Y, B'fast:N, WiFi:Y, Pvt. room:Y, Locker:Y, Recep:7a-11p;
Note: luggage ok, laundry, forex, a/c, hard to find, free tea/coffee/beer!

Af-Terr Hostel, Obilicev Venac 8/5, Belgrade, Serbia;
www.belgradeinternationalhostel.com/, T:+381112631073; $13bed,
Kitchen:N, B'fast:N, WiFi:Y, Pvt. room:Y, Locker:Y, Recep:24/7;
Note: tour desk, laundry, a/c, cash only, small & central

Central Station Hostel, Karadjordjeva 87, *hostelcentralstation.com/*,
T:0112685069, *office@hostelcentralstation.com;* $23bed,
Kitchen:Y, B'fast:N, WiFi:Y, Pvt. room:Y, Locker:Y, Recep:24/7;
Note: luggage room, laundry, parking, tour desk, forex, a/c, by bus/train

Downtown Belgrade Hostel, Karadjordjeva 91, Belgrade;
downtownbelgradehostel.com/, T:0616620582, $12bed, Kitchen:Y,
downtownbelgrade@yahoo.com; B'fast:N, WiFi:Y, Pvt.room:Y, Locker:Y,
Recep:9a>11p; Note: a/c, free coffee & tea & welcome drink/beer/soup

HostelFlash, Nušićeva 3a, Belgrade, Serbia;
www.hostelflash.com/, T:+381113222778, *info@hostelflash.com;* $17bed,
Kitchen:Y, B'fast:N, WiFi:Y, Pvt. room:Y, Locker:Y, Recep:24/7;

Note: resto/bar/café, prkng, tour desk, forex, central, laundry, a/c, c.c. ok

Hostel Centar, Gavrila Principa 46a, Belgrade, Serbia; *www.hostelcentar.com*, T:(0)113619686; $17bed, Kitchen:Y, B'fast:N, WiFi:Y, Pvt. room:Y, Locker:Y, Recep:24/7;
Note: bar/café, bikes, forex, luggage room, laundry, a/c, c.c. ok

Tash Inn Hostel, 61 Bulevar Kralja Aleksandra, Belgrade, Serbia; *www.tash-inn.com*, T:(0)113230029, *tashinn.hostel@gmail.com;* $16bed, Kitchen:Y, B'fast:N, WiFi:Y, Pvt. room:Y, Locker:Y, Recep:ltd;
Note: wheelchair ok, tour desk, luggage room, a/c, central

Hostelche Hostel, Kralja Petra St. #8, 1st Fl, Apt. #7, Belgrade, Serbia; *www.hostelchehostel.com*, T:0638379461, *hostelchehostel@gmail.com;* $20bed, Kitchen:Y, B'fast:N, WiFi:Y, Pvt. room:Y, Locker:Y, Recep:24/7;
Note: age limit 45, free tour, travel desk, laundry, ac/heat, small, central

Hostel Captain, Kapetan Mišina 16, Belgrade, Serbia; *www.hostelcaptain.com/*, T:0112181819, *office@hostelcaptain.com;* $20bed, Kitchen:Y, B'fast:N, WiFi:Y, Pvt. room:Y, Locker:Y, Recep:ltd;
Note: bar, lounge, luggage room, forex, good location

Red Door Hostel, No.60 Gavrila Principa St., Belgrade, Serbia; *reddoorhostel.org/*, T:+381116642057, *reddoorhostel@gmail.com*; $17bed, Kitchen:Y, B'fast:Y, WiFi:Y, Pvt. room:Y, Locker:Y, Recep:ltd;
Note: luggage room, laundry, tour desk, a/c, near train & bus

In Old Shoes, Brankova 18, 2nd Fl, Apt 5, Belgrade, Serbia; *www.inoldshoes.com*, T:+381112183650, *info@inoldshoes.com*; $16bed, Kitchen:Y, B'fast:N, WiFi:Y, Pvt. room:Y, Locker:Y, Recep:9a>12m;
Note: lift, TV, tour desk, a/c, central, lights & curtains for bunks

Belcity Hostel, Stojana Protica 11, Belgrade, Serbia; *www.belcityhostel.com*, T:0112433136, *belcityhostel@gmail.com*;

$14bed, Kitchen:Y, B'fast:$, WiFi:Y, Pvt. room:Y, Locker:Y, Recep:24/7;
Note: bar, lounge, luggage ok, laundry, tour desk, a/c, c.c. ok, balcony

NIS is Serbia's number three city and the largest in southern Serbia. While that may seem rather mundane, Constantine the Great was also born here, as was Justin I who founded the Byzantine Justinian Dynasty, and Attila the Hun once destroyed the town. When the Serbs in Nis attempted to achieve their freedom from the Ottoman Turks in 1809, the local commander ordered an array of skulls to be displayed as a deterrent. That today is one of the tourist attractions. There is also an Ottoman fortress, a 5th C. Byzantine crypt and a Nazi concentration camp.

www.geckogo.com/Guide/Serbia/Belgrade-District/Nis/

The Garden Hostel, Vojislava Ilica 12, Nis, Serbia;
www.thegarden.rs/, T:+38118236165, *thegarden@live.com*; $14bed, Kitchen:N, B'fast:N, WiFi:Y, Pvt. room:Y, Locker:N, Recep:24/7;
Note: luggage ok, laundry, prkng, wh/chair ok, walk to center, family

Hostel Kosmopolit, Anastasa Jovanovica 15, Nis, Serbia;
hostelkosmopolit.com/, T:063472705, *hostelkosmopolit@hotmail.com*
$14bed, Kitchen:Y, B'fast:$, WiFi:Y, Pvt. room:Y, Locker:Y, Recep:24/7;
Note: bar, parking, tour, luggage room, a/c, coffee & tea, not central

Hostel Nis, Dobricka 3A, Nis, Serbia;
www.hostelnis.rs/, T:+38118513703, *hostelnis@sezampro.rs*; $16bed, Kitchen:Y, B'fast:$, WiFi:Y, Pvt. room:Y, Locker:Y, Recep:24/7;
Note: bar, tour desk, luggage room, c.c. ok

NOVI SAD is the "Athens of Serbia," or so it has the reputation. It is also Serbia's second city, and capital of the province of Vojvodina. Located in the northernmost corner of the country the province and city have always been culturally mixed between Germans, Hungarians, and Serbs. Petrovaradin Fortress reflects Novi Sad's status as a military frontier against the Ottomans. Tourism is on the rise, and the July EXIT festival is a big deal, now one of Europe's major summer events.

you.travel/Novi_Sad

Nikola's Place, Njegoševa, Novi Sad , Serbia;
www.accomodationnovisad.com/, T:(0)63581732; $13bed,
Kitchen:N, B'fast:N, WiFi:Y, Pvt. room:Y, Locker:N, Recep:24/7;
Note: luggage room, laundry, tour desk

Hostel Podbarra, Djordja Rajkovica 28, Novi Sad, Serbia;
www.hostel-novisad.com/, T:+38121551991, *hostelpodbarra@gmail.com;*
$12bed, Kitchen:Y, B'fast:N, WiFi:Y, Pvt. room:Y, Locker:N,
Recep:24/7;
Note: close to center, smoking allowed, café, luggage room, a/c, c.c. ok

Hostel Sova, Ilije Ognjanovica 26, Novi Sad, Serbia;
www.hostelsova.com/, T:+38216615230, *kontakt@hostelsova.com;*
$13bed, Kitchen:Y, B'fast:N, WiFi:Y, Pvt.room:Y, Locker:Y, Recep:24.7;
Note: laundry, luggage room, parking, smoky, good location

Downtown NoviSad Hostel, Njegoseva 2 / II Fl, Novi Sad, Serbia;
hostelnovisad.com/, T:0641920342, *downtownnovisad@yahoo.com;*
$11bed, Kitchen:Y, B'fast:N, WiFi:Y, Pvt. room:Y, Locker:N, Recep:ltd;
Note: no lift, live-in staff, good location, hard to find, forex, free drink

SUBOTICA is the other city, besides Novi Sad, of the Vojvodina region of Serbia, far up in the northern corner of the country. And like Novi Sad, it is multi-ethnic, Hungarians forming the majority. Unlike much of Serbia, there is some interesting architecture, including Art Nouveau style. This wouldn't be a bad place to cross a border.

www.suboticagis.rs/

Incognito Hostel, Huga Badaliceva 3rd Street, Subotica, Serbia;

hostel-subotica.com/, T:062666674, *info@hostel-subotica.com;* $13bed, Kitchen:Y, B'fast:$, WiFi:Y, Pvt. room:Y, Locker:Y, Recep:>6p; Note: cash only, resto/bar, parking, luggage room, a/c, central

23) Slovakia

The nation that is now Slovakia (long form = "Slovak Republic"), enters the history books during the fifth and sixth centuries around the same time that the Roman Empire was falling and the entire continent of Europe was entering a period of intense migration. It was part of several of the earliest Slavic states to coalesce as "Samo's kingdom" and Greater Moravia. After that it was an important part of the Kingdom of Hungary and the Austrian-Habsburg Empire, then Czechoslovakia, before finally achieving independence last century. The Czech and Slovak republics separated in 1993, but are still close politically. Today Slovakia is a market-oriented multi-party capitalist democracy with a bright future. Tourism is based on medieval towns and castles, natural landscapes, and ski resorts. Slovak is the (main) language, Euro is currency and the phone code is +421.

www.slovakia.travel

BRATISLAVA is Slovakia's capital and largest city and is known variously throughout history as Pressburg, Presporik and Pozsony. Bratislava's moment in the spotlight came when the Hungarian capital was relocated here following the Ottoman Empire's occupation of Budapest in 1526. This period lasted more than three hundred years from the sixteenth to nineteenth centuries. Prior to WWI and Czechoslovakia's creation, the Slovak population in Pressburg was less than one in five, the remainder German and Hungarian. After WWII the population was 90% Slovak and the name was Bratislava. Communist Warsaw Pact troops occupied the city during Prague Spring of 1968, and it wasn't until the Velvet Revolution of 1989 that Communism was defeated. The Velvet Divorce separated the two countries in 1993. Today Old Town and Bratislava Castle are major tourist attractions. It is only 40mi/60km from Vienna, Austria.

visit.bratislava.sk/en/

Hostel Blues, Špitálska 2205/2, Staré Mesto-Bratislava I, Slovakia; *www.hostelblues.sk*, T:0905204020, *bookings@hostelblues.sk;* $21bed, Kitchen:Y, B'fast:N, WiFi:Y, Pvt. room:Y, Locker:Y, Recep:24/7;
Note: bar/café, lift, free tour/info, laundry, luggage ok, TV

Downtown Backpacker Hostel, Panenská 680/31, Bratislava, Slovakia; *www.backpackers.sk/en/*, T:0254641191, *info@backpackers.sk;* $21bed, Kitchen:Y, B'fast:$, WiFi:Y, Pvt. room:Y, Locker:Y, Recep:24/7;
Note: resto/bar/café, tour desk, luggage ok, laundry, c.c. ok, old town

Art Hostel Taurus, Zámocká 24, Staré Mesto-Bratislava 1, Slovakia; *hostel-taurus.com/*, T:0220722401, *art.hostel.taurus@gmail.com;* $19bed, Kitchen:N, B'fast:Y, WiFi:Y, Pvt. room:Y, Locker:Y, Recep:24/7;
Note: parking, luggage ok, laundry, bikes, c.c. ok. a/c, no alcohol

Hostel Possonium, Šancová 3996/20, Bratislava-Old Town, Slovakia; *www.possonium.sk*, T:0220720007, *info@possonium.sk*, $21bed, Kitchen:Y, B'fast:$, WiFi:Y, Pvt. room:Y, Locker:Y, Recep:24/7;
Note: bar, parking, luggage room, laundry, c.c. ok, not central, nr train

Hostel Spirit, Vančurova 1694/1, Bratislava - Nové Mesto, Slovakia; *www.hotelgallery.eu/*, T:0254777561, *info@hotelpirit.sk;* $31bed, Kitchen:N, B'fast:Y, WiFi:Y, Pvt. room:Y, Locker:N, Recep:24/7;
Note: parking, laundry, luggage ok, safe deposit, nice architecture

Patio Hostel, Špitálska 2196/35, Staré Mesto-Bratislava, Slovakia; *www.patiohostel.com/*, T:0252925797; $19bed, Kitchen:Y, B'fast:$, WiFi:Y, Pvt. room:Y, Locker:Y, Recep:24/7;
Note: bar, parking, laundry, luggage ok, c.c. ok, , TV, central

A1 Hostel Bratislava, Heydukova 2138/1, Bratislava-Staré Mesto; *a1hostelbratislava.com/*, T:0944280288, *A1Bratislava@gmail.com;* $20bed, Kitchen:Y, B'fast:N, WiFi:Y, Pvt. room:Y, Locker:Y, Recep:ltd;

Note: parking, bikes, laundry, luggage OK, near center

Hotel Plus, Bulharská 1743/72, Bratislava, Ružinov-Ružinov, Slovakia; *www.hotelyplus.sk*, T:0243426350, *travel@hotelyplus.sk*, $14bed, Kitchen:N, B'fast:N, WiFi:Y, Pvt. room:Y, Locker:N, Recep:24/7; Note: resto/bar, parking, forex, tour desk, laundry, luggage ok, c.c. ok

24) Slovenia

Bounded by Italy and Austria to the west and north, with Hungary and Croatia to the east and south, Slovenia has always been the most western of the Slavic Balkan countries. It is also one of the most diverse, with a Slavic language mutually unintelligible to its neighboring South Slavs, and significant dialectical differences within the country. That's because it was one of the first on the scene, and so was oriented toward Catholicism and the Western Slavs, before the Magyars separated them. They were conquered by Rome, Huns, Lombards, Charlemagne, and Magyars, before the Slovenes finally established their own Slovene identity. The Habsburgs and Austria-Hungary still dominated, though, until Slovenia's joining with South Slav states to form Yugoslavia after WWI. There they were first out the door, too, drawing up plans for independence in 1987, long before the Berlin Wall fell. They were fully independent by 1991. The country has coast, mountains, forests and plains, with weather to match. Nature figures prominently in tourist activities, and casinos, too. Euro is currency, Slovene is the language; the calling code is +386.

www.geckogo.com/Guide/Slovenia/

BLED is best known for the glacial lake of the same name, summer home to princes, kings, and dictators. There is a castle and and an island in the middle of the lake which contains a church. Before that there was a shrine to the Slavic goddess of love and fertility. Hmmm… Try the *kremma rezina*, a local pastry.

www.geckogo.com/Guide/Slovenia/Bled/

Bled B.P. Hostel, Grajska cesta 21, Bled, Slovenia;

www.bled-hostel.com, T:(0)40332706, $24bed, Kitchen:N, B'fast:$, WiFi:Y, Pvt. room:N, Locker:Y, Recep:ltd; Note: resto/bar, luggage room, travel desk, parking, castle & lake

Castle Hostel 1004, Grajska cesta 22, Bled, Slovenia; *www.hostel1004.com/*, T:(0)31523056, *castle.1004@gmail.com;* $26bed, Kitchen:N, B'fast:$, WiFi:Y, Pvt. room:N, Locker:Y, Recep:24/7; Note: bar, travel desk, luggage room, laundry, central

BOVEC is a town up in the Julian Alps on the northwest border with Italy, though historically it was most influenced by Germans. There is a national park nearby.

www.bovec.org/en

Adrenaline-Check Open Air Hostel, Soca 38, Bovec, Slovenia; *adrenaline-check.com*, T:+38641383662; *info@adrenaline-check.com*, $12bed, Kitchen:Y, B'fast:$, WiFi:Y, Pvt. room:N, Locker:N, Recep:ltd; Note: bar, parking, tour desk, natural setting, pitch tent ok

CELJE is the third-largest town in Slovenia. With distant roots in the proto-European Halstatt culture, Celje has been ruled by Celts, Greeks, and especially Romans (it was founded by Emperor Claudius as Claudia Celeia) before becoming the small Slavic city that it is today. More recently it has been a bone of contention between Germans and Slavs, with extreme atrocities in WWII. Things are calmer now, and sights include a 13th century monastery and 16th century palace.

www.geckogo.com/Guide/Slovenia/Celje-1/

MCC Hostel, Mariborska Cesta 2, Celje, Slovenia; *www.mc-celje.si/en/*, T:+386(0)34908742, *mcc.hostel@mc-celje.si;* $24bed, Kitchen:N, B'fast:N, WiFi:Y, Pvt. room:Y, Locker:Y, Recep:ltd; Note: bar, luggage room, laundry, central

IZOLA ("island") is on the small bit of coast that Slovenia can call its own (since Italy apparently hogged most of it in the area). It's no longer an island, but it's long been a tourist destination because of its hot springs. Summers are lively, with concerts and festivals.

www.virtualtourist.com/travel/Europe/Slovenia/Izola_Obcina/

Hostel Stara Sola, Korte 74, 6310 Izola, Slovenia;
www.hostel-starasola.si/, T:(0)56421114, *info@hostel-starasola.si;*
$22bed, Kitchen:Y, B'fast:$, WiFi:Y, Pvt. room:Y, Locker:Y, Recep:>8p;
Note: parking, a/c, c.c. ok, remote location 5mi/8km to town

LJUBLJANA is the capital and largest city of Slovenia. This is where Eastern Europe meets Western, and Northern Europe meets Southern. It is documented from the 12th century and was part of the Habsburg Empire by 1335, where it would remain until 1797. It was briefly a Napoleonic city before returning to Austria, all of which crumbled down in WWI. After that it joined the Yugoslavian confederation until independence in 1991. But that's politics, not culture(s). Located at the transit point between Romance, Germanic and Slavic cultures, it has always been something of a crossroads. There have always been multiple languages, German and Italian in addition to the Slavic.

There is a castle in both Germanic and Roman styles, from both classic and Renaissance periods. The Town Hall, Cathedral, and others are also noted for their architecture, though after an earthquake in 1895 much of Ljubljana has a modern, yet tasteful, appearance. Museums include the National Museum of Slovenia, the Slovenian Museum of Natural History, the National Gallery, and the Gallery of Modern Art. The city has a thriving scene for arts and culture, including a subculture. Sidewalk cafes line the river. It's a little peach of a city, almost reminds me of Tallinn.

www.visitljubljana.com/

Zeppelin Hostel, Slovenska cesta 47, Ljubljana, Slovenia;
www.zeppelinhostel.com/, T:059191427, *info@zeppelinhostel.com;*
$29bed, Kitchen:Y, B'fast:Y, WiFi:Y, Pvt.room:N, Locker:Y,
Recep:>10p;
Note: laundry, TV, push-button showers, central

Fluxux Hostel, Tomšičeva 4, Ljubljana, Slovenia;
www.fluxus-hostel.com/en, T:+38612515760, *info@fluxus-hostel.com;*
$27bed, Kitchen:Y, B'fast:N, WiFi:Y, Pvt. room:Y, Locker:N, Recep:ltd;
Note: few baths, laundry, c.c. ok, advisal arrival time, central, few staff

H2OSTEL, Petkovškovo nabrežje 47, Ljubljana, Slovenia;
www.h2ohostel.com/, T:+38641662266, *info@h2ohostel.com;* $22bed,
Kitchen:Y, B'fast:N, WiFi:Y, Pvt.room:Y, Locker:Y, Recep:>11p;
Note: advise arrival time, laundry, free linens, luggage room, on river

Alibi M14 Hostel, Miklošičeva cesta 14, Ljubljana, Slovenia;
www.alibi.si/, T:(0)12322770, +38612511244, *info@alibi.si;* $25bed,
Kitchen:Y, B'fast:N, WiFi:Y, Pvt. room:Y, Locker:Y, Recep:9a>10p;
Note: laundry, luggage room, TV, city tour, c.c. ok, central, no lift

Aladin Hostel, Tugomerjeva 56, Ljubljana, Slovenija;
www.aladin-hostel.com/, T:(0)41666477, *bookings@aladin-hostel.com,*
$24bed, Kitchen:Y, B'fast:N, WiFi:Y, Pvt. room:Y, Locker:N,
Recep:ltd;
Note: luggage ok, free linen, laundry, games, TV, c.c. ok, bit far

MARIBOR is Slovenia's second-largest city with almost 100,000 inhaitants. Historically Austrian German, and with a famous Jewish quarter, the last century saw major disputes over ownership of the territory between Germans and Slavs. After Slovene independence in 1991 and incorporation into the EU, Maribor concentrated on small businesses and tourism. There is a castle, winter sports, and medieval architecture. The scenic Old Town lines the Drava River.

maribor-pohorje.si/

Hostel Pekarna, Ob železnici 16, Maribor, Slovenia;
www.mkc-hostelpekarna.si, T:+386(0)59180880; *hostelpekarna@mkc.si;*
$22bed, Kitchen:N, B'fast:$, WiFi:Y, Pvt. room:N, Locker:Y, Recep:ltd
Note: bar, parking, laundry, a/c, c.c. ok, bike rent, central

PIRAN, like Izola, is also in that narrow strip of land that Slovenia calls its coastline. Like elsewhere there were population transfers between Slovenes and Italians after WWII. The medieval architecture here is sublime.

www.geckogo.com/Guide/Slovenia/Piran/

Alibi B14, Bonifacijeva ulica 14, 6330 Piran, Slovenia;
www.alibi.si/, T:(0)31363666, *piran@alibi.si*; $33bed,
Kitchen:N, B'fast:N, WiFi:Y, Pvt. room:Y, Locker:Y, Recep:ltd;
Note: luggage room, c.c. ok, checkin at B11, central, beach

POSTOJNA is located in an area of karst landscape and full of caves, including the most famous, Postojna Cave. Nearby Prejdama Castle is built in the mouth of a cave.

www.geckogo.com/Guide/Slovenia/Postojna/

Hotel & Hostel Sport, Kolodvorska c.1, Trzaska c.22, Postojna;
www.sport.hostel.com/, T:+38657202244; $26bed, Kitchen:Y,
B'fast:Y, WiFi:Y, Pvt. room:Y, Locker:N, Recep:24/7;
Note: bar, laundry, tour desk, bike rent, c.c. ok, near train/bus, center

RUSE is a small town near Maribor. There is a historical church, once destroyed by Ottoman Turks, and then rebuilt. You're in rural Slovenia here.

www.geckogo.com/Guide/Slovenia/Ruse/

Hostel Vetrnica, Mariborska cesta 31, Ruse, Slovenia;
www.hotel-veter.si, T:+386(0)266900, *info@hotel-veter.si*; $26bed,
Kitchen:N, B'fast:$, WiFi:Y, Pvt. room:N, Locker:N, Recep:24/7;
Note: hotel w/dorms, resto/bar, prkng, wh/chair ok, forex, a/c, c.c. ok

25) Turkey

The area now called Turkey, i.e. the Anatolian peninsula, is one of the cradles of civilization. In addition to all the prehistoric people documented in the archeological record, there are the historical Greeks, Hittites, Chaldeans, Phrygians, Romans, Armenians, Galatians, Ephesians, and... You get the idea. So when the Seljuk Turks brought their little dog-and-pony show into town from Asia in the 11th century, all those people didn't just up and skedaddle. They did what people do. You know. And for the most part they became "Turks," thereby turning an oriental dark-skinned straight-haired people into a race that looks a whole lot like you and me, except for the funny hats and clothes. They didn't fare so well against their homeboy Mongols, but the Ottomans came back in their stead. The rest is history.

The Ottomans proceeded to rule over one of the largest empires the world has ever seen, stretching north almost to Vienna and east to the Maghrib from their Mideast base. Their success was their undoing, though, that and the unbridled rise of the newly-industrialized Europe. In WWI they almost lost it all, until Mustapha Kemal reclaimed the central core for Turks themselves, and decimated Armenians in the process, one of the world's worst genocides. Turkey nowadays is in good shape to rejoin Europe as an economic player and peacefully lead an Islamic world increasingly militarized and dangerous. It's good enough for tens of millions of tourists every year. Turkish is the language; currency is *lira* (TRY); calling code is +90.

www.goturkey.com/

ANTALYA is a city of about a million souls and is Turkey's main sea resort. It dates back to the Roman era and was a major Byzantine city. Kaleici is the historic center of the city. Major tourist sights include Hadrian's Gate from the Roman era. Beaches and winter sports are both within the nearby region. It is well connected by land and air. Monuments include an ancient tower and a Seljuq mosque dating from 1250. Yivli Minare is a former Byzantine church converted into a Seljuq mosque and now home to the local archaeological museum.

www.antalya.fm/

Sabah Pansiyon, Old Town (Kaleici) Kilincaslan, nr Broken Minaret; *www.sabahpansiyon.com,* T:02422475345, *sabahpansiyon@yahoo.com;* $17bed, Kitchen:N, B'fast:Y, WiFi:Y, Pvt. room:Y, Locker:N, Recep:ltd; Note: resto/bar, travel info, luggage room, bike rent, forex, a/c, c.c. ok

Hotel Blue Sea Garden, Muratpaşa Hesapçı Sok. 65, Antalya, Turkey; *hotelblueseagarden.com,* T:02422488213, *info@hotelblueseagarden.com;* $22bed, Kitchen:N, B'fast:Y, WiFi:Y, Pvt. room:Y, Locker:N, Recep:ltd; Note: resto/bar, wheelchair ok, parking, travel info, a/c, c.c. ok

Jungle Bells Hostel, Deniz mahallesi, ucbuk mevkii, Adrasan, Antalya; *www.junglebellshostel.com,* T:02428831424, *info@junglebellshostel.com;* $21bed, Kitchen:N, B'fast:Y, WiFi:Y, Pvt. room:Y, Locker:N, Recep:ltd; Note: 90km from Antalya, resto/bar, travel info, a/c, c.c. ok, near beach

BODRUM, formerly Halicarnassus, was once part of an area called Caria ruled by one Mausolus (mausoleum, get it?), the tomb for whom was one of the seven wonders of the ancient world. It was finally destroyed by earthquakes and many of its stones used by Crusaders to build the Castle of Bodrum. Today tourism has largely displaced fishing and sponge diving as the main driver of the local economy; lucky for us.

www.bodrum.com/

Hostel Kalender, Gumbet mah, Ayaz Cad No: 50, Gumbet Bodrum; *www.hotelkalender.com.* T:02523193310, *op@hotelkalender.com;*

$20bed, Kitchen:N, B'fast:Y, WiFi:Y, Pvt. room:Y, Locker:N, Recep:24/7;
Note: resto/bar, pool, parking, tour desk, luggage room, a/c, c.c. ok, forex

Bodrum Backpackers, 37B Ataturk Cad., Bodrum, Turkey; *bodrumbackpackers.net/*, T:02523132762, *info@bodrumbackpackers.net;*
$17bed, Kitchen:N, B'fast:Y, WiFi:Y, Pvt. room:Y, Locker:N, Recep:ltd;
Note: resto/bar, games, laundry, luggage ok, terrace, close to beach, party

FETHIYE is located on the site of the ancient Lycian/Luwian city of Telemossos, which passed to the Persians, then to the Greeks as Makri. It was renamed Fethiye and repopulated with Turks (and other Muslims) from Greece during the population transfers following WWI. There is a ferry to the Greek island of Rhodes here as well as sea links to Izmir and Istanbul. There are rock tombs and sarcophagi dating from the 5th–4th century BC. There is also a ruined Byzantine fortress on a nearby hill. Currently it is very popular with Britons, both for tourism and retirement.

www.justturkey.org/turkey/fethiye/fethiye-city.asp

V-Go's Hotel/G.H., 2 Karagozler, Fevzi Cakmak Cd., #109-111; *www.v-gohotel.com*, T:+902526125409; $16bed, Kitchen:N, B'fast:Y, WiFi:Y, Pvt. room:Y, Locker:N, Recep:24/7;
Note: resto/bar/club, pool, tour desk, luggage room, a/c, walk>town

Fethiye Guesthouse, 1. Karagozler, Fevzi Cakmak Cd, no 57, Fethiye; *www.fethiyeguesthouse.com*, 02526122711, *info@fethiyeguesthouse.com;*
$14bed, Kitchen:N, B'fast:Y, WiFi:Y, Pvt. room:Y, Locker:N, Recep:24/7;
Note: free bus shuttle, tour desk, parking, luggage room, a/c, by marina

Yildrim Hostel, 37 Fethiye Mugla, Karagozler Fevzi, Çakmak Cad; *yildirimguesthouse.com/*, T:02526144627, *info@yildirimguesthouse.com;*
$13bed, Kitchen:N, B'fast:Y, WiFi:Y, Pvt. room:Y, Locker:N, Recep:24/7;

Note: parking, tour desk, a/c, c.c. ok, cash only

Freah Pension/Monica's Place, 2. Karagozler Ordu, Cad. 21, Fethiye; *www.ferahpension.com/*, T:02526142816, *ferahpension@hotmail.com;* $22bed, Kitchen:N, B'fast:Y, WiFi:Y, Pvt. room:Y, Locker:Y, Recep:24/7;
Note: café/resto/bar, TV, pool, tour desk, forex, luggage room, a/c, c.c. ok

Ideal Pension, 1.Karagözler Zafer Cad., No:1, Fethiye, Turkey; *www.idealpension.net,* T:02526141981, *idealpension@hotmail.com*; $10bed, Kitchen:N, B'fast:Y, WiFi:Y, Pvt. room:Y, Locker:N, Recep:24/7;
Note: resto/bar, parking, tour desk, luggage room, laundry, long-stay perks

GOREME is a town in the Cappadocia region of central Turkey and the center of the tourism industry of the region, based on and around the "hoodoo"/"fairy chimney" rock formations which define the region. These are formations in which a hard upper stratum has formed a cap over softer strata, which have then been weathered away and frequently carved out for utilitarian purposes, especially clandestine Christian churches in the era in which that was subversive. It's surreal and imaginations have gone wild to promote it, most often comparing it to the "yabba-dabba-doo" landscape of Fred Flintstone's Bedrock City. It is a UNESCO World Heritage site. Hostels are of good quality and good value.

www.justturkey.org/turkey/goreme/

Nomad Cave Hostel, Goreme Kasabasi Nevsehir, Goreme, Turkey; *www.nomadcavehotel.com*, T:03842712204; $11bed, Kitchen:N, B'fast:Y, WiFi:Y, Pvt. room:N, Locker:Y, Recep:ltd;
Note: restaurant, parking, laundry, luggage room, cave rooms

Dream Cave Hotel, Orta Mahalle Asker Çikmazi, Kanyolu N:2, Goreme; *falconcavesuites.com/*, T:03842712135, *info@falconcavesuites.com;*

$13bed, Kitchen:N, B'fast:Y, WiFi:Y, Pvt. room:Y, Locker:N, Recep:24/7;
Note: resto/bar, prkng, forex, laundry, luggage ok, coffee/tea, cave room

Paradise Caves & Hotel, Muze yolu cd, Celle sk #24, Goreme, Turkey; *paradisecavepension.com*, T:03842712248, $8bed, Kitchen:N, B'fast:Y, *book@paradisecavepension.com;* WiFi:Y, Pvt. room:Y, Locker:Y, Recep:ltd; Note: parking, laundry, luggage, c.c. ok

Nirvana Cave Hotel, Gafelli Mah. Cevizler Sok. #9, Goreme (Nevsehir); *www.nirvanacave.com*, T:03842713004, *info@nirvanacave.com;* $6bed, Kitchen:N, B'fast:Y, WiFi:Y, Pvt. room:Y, Locker:N, Recep:24/7;
Note: bar, parking, pool, luggage room, wheelchair ok

Star Cave Hotel Pension, Isalli mah. Isalli cad. no:15, Goreme, Turkey; *starcavecappadocia.com*, T:03842712357, *star@starcavecappadocia.com;* $14bed, Kitchen:N, B'fast:Y, WiFi:Y, Pvt. room:Y, Locker:N, Recep:24/7;
Note: bar, parking, forex, laundry, luggage room, c.c. ok

Rock Valley Pension, Isheli Mah, Içeridere Sok, Goreme, Turkey; *rockvalleycappadocia.com/*,T:03842712153,$14bed, Kitchen:N, B'fast:Y, *info@rockvalleycappadocia.com;* WiFi:Y, Pvt. room:Y, Recep:24/7;
Note: near bus, bar, parking, TV, tour desk, luggage room, laundry, pool

ISTANBUL sits at the head of modern Turkey, and is one of the world's great cities. It might not be like the old days in command of an empire, but it ain't bad. Its glory days started as Constantine's "New Rome" in 330 AD for over a hundred years, and then continued as the Byzantine capital of Constantinople for a millennium, before becoming the Ottoman capital for almost five hundred years. Nowadays it's a pleasantly huge city, more sympathetic than most of its size, surrounded by water, easily walkable and not expensive. Landmarks include the Blue Mosque, Hagia Sophia, Topkapi Palace, and many many more, too many to mention… but I'll try.

How about the Seraglio, the Çinili Kiosk (Pavilion of Tiles), the Audience Chamber (Arzodası), the Hirkaiserif, the Baghdad Kiosk, the Beylerbey Palace, the Dolmabahçe Palace, the Çeragan Palace, the Grand Bazaar and the Yıldız Palace, for starters? That should keep you busy. It also contains a huge number of backpackers' hostels, generally of very good quality (but don't look for the kitchen; I guess it's not a guy thing).

www.istanbultrails.com/

Tulip GuestHouse, Süleymaniye Mh İstanbul Üniversitesi 2, Fatih; *www.tulipguesthouse.com*, T:02125176509, *info@tulipguesthouse.com;* $20bed, Kitchen:Y, B'fast:Y, WiFi:Y, Pvt. room:Y, Locker:Y, Recep:24/7;
Note: parking, laundry, luggage room, c.c. ok, roof-top-terrace, old city

Second Home Hostel, Hoca Paşa Mh. Ebussuut Cad. 19, Sirkeci; *www.secondhomehostel.com/*, T:02125125790; $17bed, Kitchen:Y, B'fast:Y, WiFi:Y, Pvt. room:Y, Locker:N, Recep:24/7;
Note: 5th fl. no lift, restaurant, laundry, TV, basement dorm, central

Metropolis Hostel, Süleymaniye Mh., İstanbul Ünv. 24, Istanbul; *metropolishostel.com/*, T:02125181822, *info@metropolishostel.com;* $22bed, Kitchen:N, B'fast:Y, WiFi:Y, Pvt. room:Y, Locker:Y, Recep:ltd;
Note: 2N min., rooftop rest/bar, forex, parking, travel info, a/c, central

Agora Guest House, Akbiyik Cad.Amiral Tafdil sk.# 6 Sultanahmet; *www.agoraguesthouse.com*, 02124585547, *info@agoraguesthouse.com;* $20bed, Kitchen:N, B'fast:Y, WiFi:Y, Pvt.room:Y, Locker:N, Recep:24/7;
Note: ages 18-50, resto/bar, forex, forex, prkng, hard to find, a/c, c.c. ok

Bada Bing Hostel, Müeyyedzade Mh. Serçe Sokak 6, Istanbul; *www.badabinghostel.com*, T:02122494111, *info@badabinghostel.com;*

$19bed, Kitchen:Y, B'fast:Y, WiFi:Y, Pvt. room:Y, Locker:Y, Recep:24/7;
Note: ages 17-50, bar, laundry, luggage room, forex, c.c. ok, non-touristy

Rapunzel Hostel, Bereketzade Mh. Bereketzade Cami Sokak 3, Istanbul; *www.rapunzelistanbul.com*, T:02122925034, *info@rapunzelistanbul.com*; $24bed, Kitchen:N, B'fast:Y, WiFi:Y, Pvt. room:Y, Locker:Y, Recep:24/7;
Note: luggge ok, parking, forex, a/c, c.c. ok, Beyoglu area, rooftop terrace

Chambers of Boheme, Küçük Parmak Kapı Sok. 13, İstiklal Av Beyoglu; *www.chambersoftheboheme.com*, T:+902122510931; $19bed, Kitchen:Y, B'fast:Y, WiFi:Y, Pvt. room:Y, Locker:Y, Recep:24/7;
Note: luggage room, forex, travel info, c.c. ok, Taksim Sq nightlife, stairs

Taksim Sofa Hostel, Kuloglu Mh Aga Kulhani Sok5 Cukurcuma Beyoglu; *www.taksimsofahostel.com*, T:02122451053, *info@taksimsofahostel.com*; $14bed, Kitchen:Y, B'fast:Y, WiFi:Y, Pvt. room:Y, Locker:N, Recep:24/7;
Note: laundry, luggage ok, travel info, TV, tricky to find, not tourist area

Istanbul Sydney Hostel, Akbiyik Cad #42 Sultanahmet, Istanbul, Turkey; *istanbulsydneyhostel.com/*, 02125186671, *info@istanbulsydneyhostel.com*; $17bed, Kitchen:Y, B'fast:Y, WiFi:Y, Pvt. room:Y, Locker:Y, Recep:24/7;
Note: resto/bar, parking, travel info, luggage room, a/c, c.c. ok, terrace

Antique Guesthouse & Hostel, KutlugunSt. #51, 34122, Sultanahmet; *www.antiquehostel.com*, T:+902126381637, *info@antiquehostel.com*; $20bed, Kitchen:N, B'fast:Y, WiFi:Y, Pvt. room:Y, Locker:Y, Recep:24/7;
Note: bar, TV, luggage room, travel info, c.c. ok, a/c, roof-top terrace

Sultan Hostel, Akbıyık Cad. 21, Fatih, Istanbul, Turkey; *www.sultanhostel.com/*, T:02125169260, *enquiries@sultanhostel.com;* $13bed, Kitchen:N, B'fast:Y, WiFi:Y, Pvt. room:Y, Locker:Y, Recep:24/7;
Note: café, bar, parking, forex, travel info, luggage room, stairs

Eurasia Hostel, Cankurtaran Mh, Seyit Hasan Sokak 18, Fatih, Istanbul; *www.eurasiahostel.com*, T:02125181306 *info@eurasiahostel.com;* $16bed, Kitchen:Y, B'fast:Y, WiFi:Y, Pvt. room:Y, Locker:N, Recep:24/7;
Note: parking, forex, travel info, a/c, c.c. ok

Istanbul Harmony Hotel, Hocapasa mh, Hudavendigar cad 26, Istanbul; *www.istanbulharmonyhotel.com/*; T:02125188700; $14bed, Kitchen:Y, B'fast:N, WiFi:Y, Pvt. room:N, Locker:N, Recep:24/7;
Note: bar, luggage room, bikes, travel info, lift, forex, a/c, c.c. ok, dinner

Istanbul Hostel, Cankurtaran Mh, Kutlugün Sokak 35, Fatih; *www.istanbulhostel.net/*, T:02125169380; $15bed, Kitchen:Y, B'fast:Y, WiFi:Y, Pvt. room:Y, Locker:Y, Recep:24/7;
Note: resto/bar, luggage room, parking, forex, c.c. ok

Cordial House Hostel, Divanyolu Cad. Peykane, Sok. 19, Çemberlitas; *www.cordialhouse.com*, T:02125180576, *enquiries@cordialhouse.com;* $17bed, Kitchen:Y, B'fast:$, WiFi:Y, Pvt. room:Y, Locker:N, Recep:24/7;
Note: café/resto/bar, luggage room, lift, c.c. ok, easy arpt link, central

Nobel Hostel, Sultanahmet Mh Mimar Mehmet Ağa Cad 32, Istanbul; *www.nobelhostel.com*, T:02125163177, *info@nobelhostel.com;* $16bed, Kitchen:N, B'fast:Y, WiFi:Y, Pvt. room:Y, Locker:N, Recep:24/7;
Note: restaurant, luggage room, a/c, c.c. ok, views of Blue Mosque

Best Island Hostel, Kutlugün Sok. 5, Fatih, Turkey; *bestislandhostel.com/*, T:02125180170, *info@bestislandhostel.com;*

$16bed, Kitchen:N, B'fast:Y, WiFi:Y, Pvt. room:Y, Locker:Y, Recep:24/7;
Note: resto/bar, forex, laundry, luggage room, c.c. ok, rooftop views

Chillout Hostel & Café, Balyoz Sok. 3/A, Beyoğlu, Turkey; *www.chillouthostelistanbul.com*, **T:**02122494784, *chillouthc@yahoo.de;*
$13bed, Kitchen:N, B'fast:N, WiFi:Y, Pvt. room:Y, Locker:Y, Recep:24/7;
Note: café, bar, parking, laundry, luggage room, coffee & tea, basic

Sinbad Hostel, Demirci Resit Sk., Ayasofya Mh, Sultanahmet, Istanbul; *www.sinbadhostel.com/*, T:00902125182305, *sinbadhostel@yahoo.com*,
$15bed, Kitchen:N, B'fast:Y, WiFi:Y, Pvt. room:N, Locker:N, Recep:24/7;
Note: bar, parking, luggage room, c.c. ok, good location, rooftop brekkie

#bunk, Balik Sokak No. 7, Kamer Hatun Mh, Istanbul, Turkey; *www.bunkhostels.com*, T:+902122448808, *info@bunkhostels.com*;
$24bed, Kitchen:Y, B'fast:Y, WiFi:Y, Pvt. room:Y, Locker:Y, Recep:24/7;
Note: café, bar, luggage room, forex, parking a/c, c.c. ok, chic design

World House Hostel, Şahkulu Mh, Galip Dede Cad 85, Istanbul, Turkey; *worldhouseistanbul.com/*, T:02122935520, *info@worldhouseistanbul.com;* $18bed, Kitchen:N, B'fast:Y, WiFi:Y, Pvt. room:Y, Locker:Y, Recep:24/7;
Note: café, tour desk, luggage room, laundry, c.c. ok

Eastwest Hostel, Eski Cicekci Alley, N:20 Istiklal Ave, Beyoglu Istanbul; *www.eastwesthostel.com*, T:+902122444538, *info@eastwesthostel.com;*
$20bed, Kitchen:N, B'fast:Y, WiFi:Y, Pvt. room:Y, Locker:Y, Recep:24/7;
Note: coffee & tea, Taksim area, good location

Cheers Midtown, Firuzaga Mah. Bogazkesen Cd, #68 Cheers Apt; *cheersmidtown.com*, T:+902122527413, *info@cheersmidtown.com;*

$23bed, Kitchen:Y, B'fast:$, WiFi:Y, Pvt. room:Y, Locker:Y, Recep:24/7;
Note: luggage room, tour desk, forex, parking, a/c, Tophane

Han Hostel Arpt N., Değirmenbahçe Cd, Turgut Reis sok 3, Yenibosna; *www.hanhostels.com*, T:02125035800, *han@hanhostels.com;* $28bed,
Kitchen:N, B'fast:$, WiFi:Y, Pvt. room:Y, Locker:Y, Recep:24/7;
Note: café, prkng, lift, gym, luggage OK, laundry, forex, c.c. ok, by arpt

International House Hostel, Zambak sok. No: 5, Beyoglu, Istanbul; *www.ihouseistanbul.com*, T:00902122443773, *info@ihouseistanbul.com;* $18bed, Kitchen:N, B'fast:N, WiFi:Y, Pvt. room:Y, Locker:Y, Recep:24/7;
Note: lift, tour desk, TV, luggage room, c.c. ok

Mavi Guesthouse, Ishakpasa Cad., Kutlugun Sok. No:3, Istanbul; *www.maviguesthouse.com/*, T:+902125177287, *mavipans@hotmail.com;* $11bed, Kitchen:Y, B'fast:Y, WiFi:Y, Pvt. room:Y, Locker:Y, Recep:24/7;
Note: parking, tour desk, luggage room, laundry, c.c. ok, close to sights

Taksim Lounge, Katip Mustafa Celebi Mh, Mucadele cikmazi Sk 5; *www.taksimlounge.com*, 02122927759, *taksimlounge.com@hotmail.com;* $14bed, Kitchen:N, B'fast:Y, WiFi:Y, Pvt. room:Y, Locker:Y, Recep:24/7;
Note: coffee & tea, luggage room, tour desk, safe deposit, Taksim

Chambers Of The Boheme, Katip Çelebi Mh.Küçük Parmakkapı Sk 23; *www.chambersoftheboheme.com/*, T:02122510931; $18bed, Kitchen:N, B'fast:N, WiFi:Y, Pvt. room:Y, Locker:Y, Recep:24/7;
Note: no lift, tour desk, luggage room, forex, safe deposit, Taksim nights

Chillout Chengo, Hüseyinağa Mh. Halas Sokak 3, Istanbul; *cengohostelistanbul.com/*, T:02122513148, *cengohostel@hotmail.com;*

$14bed, Kitchen:N, B'fast:$, WiFi:Y, Pvt. room:Y, Locker:Y, Recep:24/7;
Note: bar, tour desk, luggage room, laundry, a/c, c.c. ok, ATM, Taksim

Planet Paprika Hostel, Şht. Muhtar Mh Taksim Akarcası Sok 3, Beyoğlu; *planetpaprika.net/*, T:02122920514, *hello@planetpaprika.net*; $20bed, Kitchen:Y, B'fast:N, WiFi:Y, Pvt. room:Y, Locker:Y, Recep:24/7;
Note: nightclub, pub crawl, cash, tour, travel desk, luggage room, laundry

Green House, İnönü Mh., Papa Roncalli Sokak 15, Şişli, İstanbul; *greenhousehostel.org/*, T:02122305839, *greenhousetaksim@gmail.com*;
$14bed, Kitchen:N, B'fast:Y, WiFi:Y, Pvt. room:Y, Locker:Y, Recep:24/7;
Note: cash, luggage room, laundry, tour desk, forex, a/c, Taksim area

Moonstar Hostel, Cankurtaran Mh. Akbıyık Caddesi 33, İstanbul; *moonstarhostel.com/*, T:02124587471, *moonstarhostel@hotmail.com*;
$16bed, Kitchen:N, B'fast:Y, WiFi:Y, Pvt. room:Y, Locker:Y, Recep:24/7;
Note: ages 18-45, bar, tour desk, laudry, a/c, c.c. ok, terrace, Sultanamet

Hush Hostel Lounge, Rasimpaşa mh, Rıhtım cd. İskele sk. #46 Kadıköy; *hushhostelistanbul.com/*; T:02164504363; $16bed, Kitchen:Y, B'fast:Y, WiFi:Y, Pvt. room:N, Locker:Y, Recep:24/7;
Note: bar, forex, luggage rm, laundry, a/c, c.c. ok, tour desk, steep hill

Pera Sultan Hotel, Keresteci Hakki Sk#22, Cankurtaran Mh Sultanahmet; *www.perasultanhotel.com/*, T:02124580087, *info@perasultanhotel.com*;
$20bed, Kitchen:N, B'fast:N, WiFi:Y, Pvt. room:Y, Locker:N, Recep:24/7;
Note: parking, tour desk, luggage room, c.c. ok, near main tourist sites

Route 39 Hostel,Mebusan Yokusu #39, 34433 Taksim Findikli Beyoglu; *route39istanbul.com*, T:+902122491901; *route39house@gmail.com;* $13bed, Kitchen:N, B'fast:Y, WiFi:Y, Pvt. room:Y, Locker:Y, Recep:24/7;
Note: dorm age >45, resto/bar/club, luggage room, laundry, forex, c.c. ok

Galata West, Bereketzade Mah., Savcibey Cikmazi #3, Galata Beyoglu; *galatawesthostel.com/*, T:+902122497218; $14bed, Kitchen:Y, B'fast:Y, WiFi:Y, Pvt. room:Y, Locker:Y, Recep:24/7;
Note: laundry, TV, tour desk, a/c, cash only, commercial district

Piya Hostel, Sultan Ahmet Mh. Akbıyık Cami Sokak 22, Fatih; *piyahostel.com/*, T:02124582060, *info@piyahostel.com*; $17bed, Kitchen:Y, B'fast:Y, WiFi:Y, Pvt. room:Y, Locker:Y, Recep:24/7;
Note: luggge room, tour desk, c.c. ok, Sultanahmet tourist area

Mavi Onur, **Küçük Ayasofya Mh, Aksakal Sokak 28, Sultanahmet;** *www.mavionurhotel.com/*, **T:+902124580690**, *mavionurhotel@gmail.com* $14bed, Kitchen:Y, B'fast:Y, WiFi:Y, Pvt. room:Y, Locker:N, Recep:24/7;
Note: dorm age limit 50 y.o., steep stairs, tourist area

Big Apple Hostel,Akbiyik cad Bayramfirin sok12, Sultanahmet, Istanbul; *www.hostelbigapple.com/*, T:02125177931, *info@hostelbigapple.com*; $21bed, Kitchen:N, B'fast:Y, WiFi:Y, Pvt. room:Y, Locker:Y, Recep:24/7;
Note: resto/bar/club/café, luggage ok, tour desk, forex, a/c, c.c. ok, prkng

Sumo Cat Hostel, Mueyyedzade Mh Luleci Hendek Cd Ali Hoca Ar; *sumocathostel.com/*, T:02122927866, *info@sumocathostel.com*; $18bed, Kitchen:Y, B'fast:Y, WiFi:Y, Pvt. room:Y, Locker:N, Recep:24/7;
Note: bar, lounge, luggage room, a/c, c.c. ok, hard to find at first

OLYMPOS was one of the main cities of the Lycian League and was added to the Roman Empire in the first century B.C. It figures in Homerian epics and was visited by Roman emperors. It was active through the Middle Ages, and then finally abandoned. Today it is known and visited not only for its ancient artifacts, but also its beautiful landscapes. It's also known for its hippie treehouses. There are no ATM's.

www.turkeytravelplanner.com/go/med/olimpos/

Saban Treehouse, Olympos Yazirkoyu, Kumluca Antalya, Olympos;
www.sabanpansion.com, T:02428921265, *info@sabanpansion.com;*
$17bed, Kitchen:N, B'fast:Y, WiFi:Y, Pvt. room:Y, Locker:N, Recep:24/7;
Note: dinner inc, resto/bar, prkng, forex, luggage ok, laundry, a/c, c.c. ok

Deep Green Bungalows, Yazir Koyu, Kumluca, Antalya, Olympos;
olymposdeepgreen.com/, T:02428921090, *info@olymposdeepgreen.com;*
$17bed, Kitchen:N, B'fast:Y, WiFi:Y, Pvt. room:Y, Locker:Y, Recep:ltd;
Note: resto/bar, tour desk, laundry, forex, a/c, c.c. ok, dinners

Olympos Orange, Yazir Koyu Olympos Mevkii, Turkey;
olymposorangepension.com/, 02428921317, *olymposorangepension.com;*
$11bed, Kitchen:N, B'fast:Y, WiFi:Y, Pvt. room:Y, Locker:N, Recep:24/7;
Note: wheelchair ok, resto/bar/club, laundry, parking, forex, a/c, c.c. ok

Bayrams Treehouses, Olympos, Kumluca, Olympos, Turkey;
www.bayrams.com, T:(009)02428921243, *olympos@bayrams.com*;
$20bed, Kitchen:N, B'fast:Y, WiFi:Y, Pvt. room:Y, Locker:N, Recep:ltd;
Note: resto/bar, prkng, forex, luggage room, laundry, a/c, c.c. ok, beach

Kadir's Yörük Top Tree House, Olympos, Antalya, Turkey;
www.kadirstreehouses.com, T:024289212, *info@kadirstreehouses*;
$16bed, Kitchen:N, B'fast:Y, WiFi:Y, Pvt. room:Y, Locker:N, Recep:ltd;
Note: resto/bar, parking, forex, laundry, c.c. ok

PAMUKKALE is a city built upon the ruins of the Roman bath city of Hierapolis. But these are not just any baths, but ones that feature travertines as part of the landscape. These are terraces formed by calcium carbonate sediments that form from the flowing thermal springs, and are strikingly beautiful, like the "cotton castles" that the name suggests. The ruins include baths, a gymnasium, an agora, and a Byzantine church. The ancient and modern cities together form a UNESCO World heritage site.

www.pamukkale.net/

Artemis Yoruk Hotel, Denizli Merkez, Atatürk Cad. 48, Denizli, Turkey; *artemisyorukhotel.com/*, T:02582722674, *info@artemisyorukhotel.com;* $12bed, Kitchen:N, B'fast:Y, WiFi:D, Pvt. room:N, Locker:N, Recep:24/7;
Note: resto/bar, prkng, left luggage, laundry, c.c. ok, pool, Jacuzzi, sauna

Hotel Dort Mevsim, Hasan Tahsin Cad no 19 Pamukkale Village DN; *www.hoteldortmevsim.com*, T:02582722009, *info@hoteldortmevsim.com;* $15bed, Kitchen:N, B'fast:$, WiFi:Y, Pvt. room:Y, Locker:N, Recep:24/7;
Note: free bus pick-up, bar, prkng, tour, tour desk, forex, a/c, c.c. ok

Kale Hotel, Atatürk Cad, Kale Mah #16, Pamukkale, Turkey; *www.otelkale.com*, T:+902582722607, *info@otelkale.com;* $9bed, Kitchen:N, B'fast:Y, WiFi:Y, Pvt. room:Y, Locker:N, Recep: 24/7;
Note: resto/bar, parking, forex, pool, luggage rm, tour desk, a/c, close

SELCUK is a base for visiting the ancient city of Ephesus, which is only a mile or so away and home of the Ephesians. Remember them? It was renamed for the original conquering Turks in the region, who arrived long before the Ottomans. It retains much of its traditional atmosphere and culture.

www.geckogo.com/Guide/Turkey/Aegean-Region/Selcuk/

Attila's Getaway, Acarlar Koyu No: 1, Selcuk, Turkey; *www.atillasgetaway.com*, T:+9002328923847, *info@atillasgetaway.com*, $11bed, Kitchen:N, B'fast:$, WiFi:Y, Pvt. room:Y, Locker:N, Recep:24/7;
Note: resto-bar, laundry, luggage room, parking, a/c, pool, shuttle to town

Anz Guest House, 1064 SK # 12, Selcuk, Turkey; *www.anzguesthouse.com*, T:(0)2328926050, *info@anzguesthouse.com*, $14bed, Kitchen:N, B'fast:Y, WiFi:Y, Pvt. room:Y, Locker:N, Recep:24/7;
Note: restaurant, luggage room, laundry, info, free bikes, walk to Ephesus

Artemis G.H./Jimmy's Place, Atatürk Mahallesi, 1016 Sk 19, Pazar Yeri; *www.artemisguesthouse.com/*, T:(+90)2328921982; $13bed, Kitchen:N, B'fast:Y, WiFi:Y, Pvt. room:Y, Locker:Y, Recep:24/7;
Note: bar, parking, forex, laundry, luggage ok, info, c.c. ok, bus transfer

Nur Pension, Zafer Mah 3004 Sk., No. 20, Selcuk, Izmir, Turkiye; *www.nur-pension.com/*; T:+902328926595; $13bed, Kitchen:Y, B'fast:Y, WiFi:Y, Pvt. room:Y, Locker:N, Recep:24/7;
Note: parking, laundry, luggage ok, a/c, bus pick-up, garden terrace

Boomerang GH, Ataturk mh, Ugur mumcu sevgi yolu 1047 sk 10; *www.boomerangguesthouse.com* T:02328924879; $14bed, Kitchen:N, B'fast:Y, WiFi:Y, Pvt. room:Y, Locker:N, Desk hr:24/7;
Note: resto/bar, parking, travel info, laundry, luggage room, a/c, shuttle

26) Ukraine

After Russia, Ukraine is the second-largest country in Europe, and it is not only vast but diverse, with Black Sea Coast, Carpathian Mountains, rivers, castles, historic urban areas, and the broad fertile fields where people make wine and folk art and not enough babies. Ukraine has a demographic crisis that some countries could (or at least **should**) only wish for, a declining fertility rate and population. How did this all begin? The history is as interesting and diverse as the countryside, all the more so because it is so recent. The best picture is that of Kiev as the center of a Slavic state founded in the 9th century led by Scandinavian Varangian "Rus" which endured for several hundred years. After the invasions of the Mongols, that proto-Ukraine was left divided between the Golden (Mongol) Horde, Lithuania, and Poland. The next major phase was in union with Russia as part of Austria-Hungary, and then as part of the USSR under Russian domination, until independence in 1991.

Of course that thumbnail sketch says nothing of the Greeks, Romans, Byzantines, Goths, Huns, or Bulgars who came before and who all moved on to other parts. And it says nothing of the Zaporozhian Cossacks, a self-styled warrior class who ruled something of a cowboy commonwealth of refugee Ukrainian serfs beyond the Pale of Polish control past the Dnieper River, called the "Cossack Hetmanate" or "Zaporozhian Host" (17th C). And it says even less about the depradations of those same Mongols still lingering long through history (to nearly 1800) as the Crimean khanate, whose economy was apparently heavily based on the trade of slaves from the Slavic lands ("slav" – "slave"), and Ukraine in particular. And it says absolutely nothing about the slights to status and sleights of hand inflicted throughout history from big brother Russia toward lil' bro' Ukraine, least of all the 1930's famines under the guise and guidance of the USSR that most likely could have been prevented and which many call genocide.

So now Ukraine is free, and still it is slow to thrive, at least demographically, the whys and wherefores of which would probably explain something about us all, and "Caucasians" in particular. Economically things are much better. After a rough early patch, things have been good the last decade and Ukraine is open for tourism. It is in fact my personal recommendation as a "starter kit" for the old USSR. No visas are required for Americans, it is linked by public transportation within and without, it is reasonably priced, AND it's big and beautiful. Embroidery is a splendid folk art in Ukraine. The Russian fleet still parks on Ukraine's coast. I don't think there was an option. Ukraine (and Russian) is the language; *hryvnia* (!?) is the currency; phone code is +380.

www.ukraine.com/

CHERNIVTSI is, along with Lviv, one of the main cultural centers of western Ukraine. Historically, the city's population has been a mixture of Ukrainians, Romanians, Jews, Germans, and Armenians, as the chief city in the territory of Bukovina. It only became part of the USSR in 1940. Situated just north of the border with Romania, Chernivtsi still has a large Romanian minority and Russians as well. It's a UNESCO world heritage site.

ua-traveling.com/en/information/chernovtsy

Tiu Chernivtsi Backpackers, 2, Sheptytskogo Apt.3, Chernivtsi, Ukraine; *www.hihostels.com.ua/*, T:+380508857049, *info@hihostels.com.ua;*
$14bed, Kitchen:Y, B'fast:N, WiFi:Y, Pvt. room:Y, Locker:Y, Recep:24/7;
Note: luggage ok, laundry, free tour, travel desk, parking, by train/center

KIEV is the capital and largest city in Ukraine, and center of Ukrainian culture, located north and central on the Dnieper River. One of the oldest cities in Eastern Europe, myths attribute its founding to the legendary Kyi and his family. Documents indicate that it was an outpost for the Khazars at the time it fell to the Varangian "Rus." Turkic Pechenegs and Kipchaks harassed it before the Mongols devastated Kiev, affecting civilization in the region for centuries. As a vassal to other empires, what Kiev lost as a regional capital it made up as a spiritual one, as an important Christian center attracting pilgrims. Growing Russification threatened it culturally, though, as Russian culture became the high one and Ukrainian the folk culture of the lower classes.

Kiev industrialized rapidly under Russian tutelage and in 1934 it became the capital of Ukraine USSR. The Nazis killed more than a half million Ukrainians in the Battle of Kiev, and more than 30,000 Jews in the aftermath, but Kiev recovered in the post-war period. The nearby Chernobyl nuclear catastrophe occurred in 1986. The tour is now a popular attraction. Others include St. Sophia Cathedral and the Monastery of the Caves. Then there are the Baroque church of St. Andrew, the ruins of the Golden Gate, the Zaborovskyy Gate, and the remains of the Desyatynna Church, or Church of the Tithes. Today Kiev is a blend of modern and ancient, green and clean. The historic center has been polished and shined. Summertime is festive.

www.visitkievukraine.com/

D'Lux Kiev Hostel, 10 Observatorna, 6 Fl, Apt 6, code 1010, Kiev; *dlux-kiev-hostel.com/*, T:+38(097)8328888, *hostel.dlux@gmail.com*,
$15bed, Kitchen:Y, B'fast:$, WiFi:Y, Pvt. room:Y, Locker:Y,
Recep:24/7;
Note: Jacuzzi, lift, luggage room, laundry, tour desk, TV, a/c, c.c. ok

Dream Hostel, Chervonoarmiis'ka St, 47, 17, Kyiv city, Ukraine; *dream-hostel.com/*, T:(066)2441447, *booking@dream-hostel.com;*
$20bed, Kitchen:Y, B'fast:$, WiFi:Y, Pvt. room:Y, Locker:N,
Recep:24/7;
Note: free tour, luggage room, laundry, parking, a/c, c.c. ok

Kiev Central Station Hostel, Gogolivska, 25 Apt 15, Kyev, Ukraine; *kievcentralstation.com/*, T: (093)7587468, *info@kievcentralstation.com;*
$14bed, Kitchen:Y, B'fast:N, WiFi:Y, Pvt. room:Y, Locker:Y,
Recep:24/7;
Note: luggage room, laundry, forex, tour desk, a/c, 6 Fl no lift

Magic Bus, Saksahans'koho St, 31, 3, Kyiv, Kyiv city, Ukraine; *magicbushostel.com/*; T:(097)3360303; $11bed, Kitchen:Y,

B'fast:N, WiFi:Y, Pvt. room:Y, Locker:Y, Recep:24/7;
Note: free tour, travel desk, laundry, tea & coffee, a/c, central

Really Central Hostel, Bogdana Khmelnitskogo St. Bldg #10, Fl 2 # 50; *www.reallycentralkiev.hostel.com/*; T:(098)2636506; $21bed, Kitchen:Y, B'fast:Y, WiFi:Y, Pvt. room:Y, Locker:Y, Recep:24/7;
Note: parking, luggage ok, laundry, free tour/info, a/c, pub crawls

LVIV (Lvov, Lwow, etc.) is Ukraine's second city and is located in the far west, close to the border with Poland, and the easiest part of Ukraine to access from the west, with convenient bus and train connections. It has historically been a center of culture for Galicia—including Jews, Ukrainians, and Poles—whose various kingdoms and incarnations it has been attached to more than any other. It also had a major German phase as a part of the Habsburg Empire from 1772-1918. In fact it only returned to the Ukraine homeland after WWII and was at the forefront of those calling for a break with communism and the Soviet Union. Now it's rapidly becoming a center for tourism. Much of the architecture dates from the 13th century. The historic center is a UNESCO world heritage site. Prices are good and the people are friendly. It's famous for its beauty. There isn't much English, but everybody speaks Russian, so that helps.

lviv.travel/en/index/

Old City Hostel, Beryndy St, 3, L'viv, L'vivs'ka oblast, Ukraine; *oldcityhostel.lviv.ua/en/*, T:0322949644, *booking@oldcityhostel.lviv.ua;* $10bed, Kitchen:Y, B'fast:N, WiFi:Y, Pvt. room:Y, Locker:Y, Recep:24/7;
Note: luggage room, laundry, tour desk, forex, central

Soviet Home Hostel, Drukars'ka St, 3, 13, L'viv, L'vivs'ka, Ukraine; *soviethomehostel.lviv.ua/*, T:0322727611, *info@soviethomehostel.lviv.ua*, $12bed, Kitchen:N, B'fast:N, WiFi:Y, Pvt. room:Y, Locker:Y, Recep:24/7;
Note: luggage room, laundry, free tour, central

Central Square Hostel, 5 Rynok Square, Lviv, Ukraine;

cshostel.com/, T:(095)2256654, *cshostel@gmail.com;* $13bed, Kitchen:Y, B'fast:N, WiFi:Y, Pvt. room:Y, Locker:Y, Recep:24/7;
Note: club, prkng, free tour/info, luggage ok, laundry, cc ok, central

Coffee Home Hostel, Javorskogo Sq. 1, Lviv, Ukraine;
coffeehomehostel.lviv.ua; T:0932399393, *coffee@homehostels.com.ua;*
$12bed, Kitchen:Y, B'fast:N, WiFi:Y, Pvt. room:Y, Locker:N, Recep:24/7;
Note: laundry, luggage room, parking

Mister Hostel, Bankivska Str. 5, Lviv, Ukraine;
www.misterhostellviv.com, T:0964798567, *misterhostel@gmail.com;*
$9bed, Kitchen:Y, B'fast:N, WiFi:Y, Pvt. room:Y, Locker:N, Recep:24/7;
Note: luggage room, laundry, tea & coffee

Cherry Hostel, Tadeusha Kostyushka St, 5 Lviv, Lvivs'ka oblast;
fruit-hostels.lviv.ua, T:(097)6055599, *cherryhostel30@gmail.com;*
$13bed, Kitchen:N, B'fast:Y, WiFi:Y, Pvt. room:N, Locker:Y Recep:24/7;
Note: luggage room, tour desk, parking, a/c, c.c. ok, center

ODESSA is Ukraine's third city and a major seaport on the Black Sea. It still shares something of a mixed Russian/Ukraine identity, and Russian is still the most common language spoken. Originally a Greek colony, it has at various times been claimed by tribal Pechenegs, the Golden Horde, the Crimean Khanate, the Grand Duchy of Lithuania, and the Ottoman Turks. It is probably most famous for the battleship Potemkin, and Sergei Eisenstein's reenactment of that famous battle and massacre.

www.odessa-guide.com/

Babushka Grand Hostel, Mala Arnauts'ka St. 60, 16, Odesa, Odes'ka;
www.babushkagrand.com, T:(063)0705535, *babushka.grand@gmail.com*,
$17bed, Kitchen:Y, B'fast:N, WiFi:Y, Pvt. room:Y, Locker:Y, Recep:24/7;

Note: luggage OK, laundry, parking, tour desk, a/c, c.c. ok, near train/bus

SEVASTOPOL is on the Crimean peninsula that juts out into the Black sea, thus making it the warmest city in Ukraine and a favorite holiday spot for ex-USSR countries. There was originally a Greek colony there, before becoming Roman then Byzantine then Ukrainian. The Russian presence is still strong, as it is elsewhere in the region, since the Russian fleet is stationed there, by mutual arrangement (after some dispute) between the two countries.

ukrainetrek.com/sevastopol-city

Funny Dolphin Hostel, yl.V.Kuchera, Bldg 5, apt.2, Sevastopol; *www.funnydolphin.hostel.com/*, T:0955013343, *funny_dolphin@mail.ru*; $18bed, Kitchen:Y, B'fast:N, WiFi:Y, Pvt. room:Y, Locker:N, Recep:ltd; Note: laundry, TV, a/c, tour info, central

About the Author

American Hardie Karges took his first extended international trip at the age of twenty-one in 1975 and traveled to his first ten countries within two years, all for less than two thousand dollars. Thus began a way of life that has taken him to some 150 countries (and counting), living and working in a dozen of them, learning several languages and trading in folk art and cottage industry products. He writes several blogs and has also published poetry, before finally deciding to write about what he knows best—travel. His first book, "Hypertravel: 100 Countries in 2 Years," was published in 2012. The full set of "Backpackers & Flashpackers" is projected to include six volumes and be completed by the end of 2013.

CENTRAL AND EASTERN EUROPE
WHITE SEA
Arkhangel'sk (Archangel)
Oulu
Umeå
GULF OF BOTHNIA
FINLAND
Trondheim
Lake Onega
Petrozavodsk
Konosha
Bergen
NORWAY
Lake Ladoga
Tampere
Turku (Åbo)
Oslo
Helsinki
SWEDEN
Åland Is.
Gulf of Finland
St. Petersburg
Vologda
Stockholm
Tallinn
Rybinsk Reservoir
Hiiumaa
ESTONIA
Lake Peipus
Novgorod
Göteborg
Saaremaa
Tartu
L. Ilmen
Yaroslavl'
Ålborg
Jönköping
Gulf of Riga
L. Pskov
Pskov
RUSSIAN FEDERATION
Nizhniy Novgorod
DENMARK
Gotland
Tver'
Århus
Riga
Liepāja
LATVIA
Moscow
Copenhagen
Malmö
BALTIC SEA
Šiauliai
Daugavpils
Panevėžys
Klaipėda
LITHUANIA
Vicebsk
Ryazan'
Kaliningrad
Kaunas
Smolensk
Hamburg
Rostock
RUSSIAN FEDERATION
Vilnius
Tula
Gdańsk
Barysau
Elbląg
Mahilëu
Bremen
Szczecin
Minsk
Olsztyn
Bryansk
Hannover
Berlin
Bydgoszcz
Toruń
Białystok
BELARUS
Orel
Poznań
Baranavičy
Babrujsk
GERMANY
Warsaw
Homel'
Voronezh
Leipzig
POLAND
Brest
Pinsk
Kursk
Dresden
Łódź
Radom
Wrocław
Lublin
Karlovy Vary
Opole
Kielce
Luts'k
Rovno
Kyiv
Prague
Zhytomyr
Nürnberg
Plzeň (Pilsen)
Kraków
Rzeszów
Kharkiv
CZECH REP.
L'viv
Poltava
České Budějovice
Brno
Ternopil'
München (Munich)
Žilina
Ivano-Frankivs'k
Vinnytsya
UKRAINE
Luhansk
Košice
Dnipropetrovs'k
Linz
Vienna
SLOVAKIA
Donets'k
Shakhty
Bratislava
Chernivtsi
Innsbruck
AUSTRIA
Miskolc
Kryvyy Rih
Bălți
Mariupol'
Rostov na Donu
Graz
Budapest
Nyíregyháza
REP. OF MOLDOVA
HUNGARY
Debrecen
Baia Mare
Chișinău
Mykolayiv
Verona
Trieste
Ljubljana
Cluj Napoca
Bacau
SLOVENIA
Zagreb
Pécs
Szeged
Arad
ROMANIA
Odesa
Sea of Azov
Venice
Rijeka
CROATIA
Kerch
Krasnodar
Bologna
Osijek
Novi Sad
Timișoara
Sibiu
Galați
Crimea
Novorossiysk
SAN MARINO
Banja Luka
BOSNIA AND HERZEGOVINA
Tuzla
Pitești
Ploiești
Sevastopol'
Florence
Belgrade
Craiova
Bucharest
Perugia
Sarajevo
Constanța
Split
SERBIA
ADRIATIC SEA
BLACK SEA
ITALY
Mostar
Niš
Pleven
Varna
Rome
Pescara
Dubrovnik
MONTENEGRO
BULGARIA
Podgorica
Sofia
Stara Zagora
Burgas
Foggia
Skopje
Plovdiv
Naples
Bari
Tirana
THE FORMER YUGOSLAV REP. OF MACEDONIA
ALBANIA
Istanbul
Thessaloníki
Sea of Marmara
Ankara
TURKEY
Bursa
TYRRHENIAN SEA
IONIAN SEA
GREECE
AEGEAN SEA
Balikesir
Izmir
0
200
400
600 km
0
200
400 mi
20°
30°
40°
50°
60°

AVE, GRAT

www.ingramcontent.com/pod-product-compliance
Lightning Source LLC
Chambersburg PA
CBHW070955040426
42443CB00007B/520
* 9 7 8 0 9 8 8 4 9 0 5 2 9 *